U.S. Army Uniforms and Equipment, 1889

U.S. Army Uniforms and Equipment, 1889

Specifications for Clothing, Camp and Garrison Equipage, and Clothing and Equipage Materials

Foreword by Jerome A. Greene

Published by the Direction of the
Quartermaster General of the Army

University of Nebraska Press
Lincoln and London

Foreword copyright 1986 by the University of Nebraska Press
Manufactured in the United States of America

The paper in this book meets the minimum requirements of American National Standard for Information Sciences — Permanence of Paper for Printed Library materials, ANSI Z39.48-1984.

First Bison Book printing: 1986
Most recent printing indicated by the first digit below:
    2   3   4   5   6   7   8   9   10

Library of Congress Cataloging-in-Publication Data
U.S. Army uniforms and equipment, 1889.
  Reprint. Originally published under title: specifications for clothing, camp and garrison equipage, and clothing and equipage materials. [Philadelphia]: Published by direction of the U.S. Quartermaster General of the Army at the Philadelphia Depot of the Quartermaster's Dept., 1889.
  1. United States. Army — Uniforms. 2. United States. Army — Equipment. I. Specifications for clothing, camp and garrison equipage, and clothing and equipage materials. II. Title: United States Army uniforms and equipment, 1889.
UC483.U18 1986   355.8'1'0973   86-6972
ISBN 0-8032-4552-1
ISBN 0-8032-9552-9 (pbk.) (alk. paper)

Originally published in 1889 by direction of the Quartermaster General of the Army at the Philadelphia Depot of the Quartermaster's Department

Foreword

By Jerome A. Greene

Publication of *Specifications for Clothing, Camp and Garrison Equipage, and Clothing and Equipage Materials* by the Quartermaster General in 1889 marked a milestone in the development of standards and specifications for clothing and equipment and the contract administration of such items by the War Department. For much of the nineteenth century the procurement and supply of military clothing and equipment was dealt with ad hoc, in a manner geared to meet immediate national exigencies. The experiences of the Mexican and Civil wars, in particular, put into sharp focus the problems in the Quartermaster Department of matériel acquisition and production. During the latter decades of the century, administrative disorder ultimately contributed to the development of procedures, represented, partly at least, by the present volume, governing the requisition and manufacture of quartermaster materials.

As defined at the time of the Civil War, the role of the Quartermaster Department was manifold: to provide "the quarters and transportation of the army; storage and transportation for all army supplies; army clothing; camp and garrison equipage; cavalry and artillery horses; fuel; forage; straw; material for bedding, and stationary." Perhaps the most difficult part of this job was the administration of clothing and equipment. Plagued by changing economic conditions during the years following the War of 1812, by understaffing, and by bureaucratic changes in supply procurement, distribution, and accountability, the Quartermaster Department had been forced in the 1820s to assume tasks beyond those traditionally dealing with transportation. In 1832 Secretary of War Lewis Cass established the Clothing Bureau within the War Department, thus further formalizing the new responsibility of the Quartermaster General.

The outbreak of the war with Mexico brought problems in clothing administration, mainly in terms of the availability and timely production of garments for use by the regular and volunteer forces fighting the war.

The primary place of manufacture was the Schuylkill Arsenal in Philadelphia, and the coming of the war strained its production capabilities. Nonetheless, the staff at Schuylkill, augmented by wartime workers, succeeded in meeting the emergency requirements. Under production guidelines, cloth, buttons, and similar appurtenances were purchased from the private suppliers and turned over to seamstresses to make into garments. Shoes were also produced at the arsenal, although many pairs were supplied under civilian contract. After the war, Schuylkill continued to manufacture clothing for the army. Aside from the emergency of the war with Mexico, procurement at Schuylkill during the 1840s and 1850s was largely successful because of the small size of the army.

The advent of the Civil War in 1861 found the circumstances of the Quartermaster Department much like those in 1846. Under the administration of Quartermaster General Montgomery C. Meigs, Schuylkill still manufactured uniforms from material purchased from private sources to supply the peacetime needs of the army. Again the coming of war pointed up the inadequacy of the system, especially after President Lincoln's call for volunteers. Nor could contracted private manufacturers satisfy the urgent need to clothe the thousands of men who took the oath of enlistment. The shortage of military clothing wrought confusion, as contractors, motivated more often by greed than by patriotism, rushed production of inferior articles. Garments purchased from civilian suppliers imitated in appearance those manufactured at the clothing depots in Philadelphia, New York, Cincinnati, and St. Louis, but usually disintegrated from poor quality or workmanship within days or weeks of issue. Profiteering was rampant. Such was the desperation of army officials to clothe the troops that General Meigs entered into agreements with European contractors to outfit large numbers of men with foreign-made clothing and equipment. As before, manufacturing standards for particular items were written into individual contracts, to be verified after production by purchasing agents for the army. Meigs tried to develop specifications to guide contract production, but the chaos of the war forced postponement of such improvements. Despite its obvious shortcomings, the existing contracting system continued through the war, although by 1865, largely because of Meigs's leadership, legislative reforms had improved the supervision of contracts and the inspection and acceptance of army goods.

Owing mainly to the slowly improving contracting system, the end of the war saw the Quartermaster Department glutted with stockpiles of clothing and equipment that would, it seemed, last for years. Damaged articles were sold and others given away, but the majority of quartermaster items were distributed among the regular forces. Most of the Civil War surplus was stockpiled at the Philadelphia Quartermaster Depot, which continued manufacturing on a limited basis. Other distribution points were at New York and Washington, D.C., although the increasing number of garrisons of the postwar army on the frontier were supplied from Jeffersonville, Indiana. Many surplus articles earmarked for the western commands were channeled through Fort Leavenworth, and in 1878 a new quartermaster depot opened at San Antonio to distribute supplies to stations in the Southwest.

As stockpiles of Civil War clothing diminished in the 1870s through depletion and deterioration, the need for production capability once more arose. In 1872 the army abruptly adopted a new uniform, although the old ones continued to be issued until supplies were exhausted (for some accessories this was well into the 1880s). Nonetheless, the suddenness of the change of pattern caught the Quartermaster Department off guard; Meigs had no opportunity to develop an orderly manufacturing process before production was to begin, and once more the formulation of specifications was delayed. Only in 1877—five years after the uniform change took effect—was Meigs able to publish the first large body of standards to guide procurement of clothing and equipment.

With the adoption of the new uniform, the army resumed clothing production in Philadelphia and also opened garment-manufacturing centers at Jeffersonville and San Francisco. Numerous items of clothing and equipage, particularly headgear, furniture, camp gear, flags, fabric, and miscellaneous goods, were produced under contract with a multitude of private firms. Other items, such as shoes, brooms, and barracks chairs, were more economically fabricated at the military prison at Fort Leavenworth, which produced items under edict of Congress. The postwar years witnessed the development of seasonal army clothing, such as overshoes, mittens, solar helmets, and cotton duck suits for use in extreme summer and winter climates. Buffalo overcoats were issued sparingly. As the great herds declined, the coats were replaced with blanket-lined canvas coats that afforded equal warmth.

Strict specifications governed the production of clothing and equipment in the years after the Civil War, regardless of manufacturer—quartermaster depot, military prison, or private contractor. This reflected in part the lessons of the wartime experience. By 1877, however, reforms in the contract system, especially in advertisement, had made it more economical than production by the government, in the eyes of Quartermaster Department officials. The manufacture of principal articles like uniforms continued at the depots in Philadelphia, Jeffersonville, and San Francisco, although throughout the 1870s and 1880s the quality of some items produced under contract improved considerably. Indeed, competition for army contracts often inspired individuals and firms to create new designs for consideration and, sometimes, adoption by the army.

Published specifications for uniforms, clothing, material, and equipment first appeared in 1877 in the Quartermaster General's annual report accompanying that of the Secretary of War. Thereafter, whenever new articles were adopted, or when pattern changes occurred, the specifications were published in the yearly report of the Quartermaster General. As changes in clothing and equipment accrued and standards became more detailed in the 1880s, the need for a comprehensive volume reflecting the status of all issue articles increased. As a result, a "book of specifications" was published by the department in the early 1880s. By 1886, after diverse changes in the dress of the army, the book was no longer reliable and needed replacement. Thus, the idea for the present volume, complete with illustrations, was conceived. Final publication came in 1889, after revisions to the manuscript at the Philadelphia Quartermaster Depot to accommodate a number of specifications recently adopted. As described by the military storekeeper, Captain John F. Rodgers, the book contained "illustrations of each article of clothing and equipage supplied by the Quartermaster's Department, drawn on scale, and specifications conforming thereto."

Issued in an extremely limited edition, *Specifications* was distributed to the officers of the Quartermaster Department, who in 1890 numbered fewer than sixty. The copy from which the present reprint was prepared surfaced among the effects of Major Lafayette E. Campbell, who served in the department during the 1880s and helped establish Fort Sam Houston, Texas, and Fort Logan, Colorado. A Civil War veteran and regular army infantry officer until his transfer into the Quartermaster Department, Campbell settled in Denver following his retirement in 1891. He died there in 1919.

Readers will find further information about the background, organization, and function of the Quartermaster Department in the following works: Chester L. Kieffer, *Maligned General: The Biography of Thomas Sidney Jesup* (San Rafael: Presidio Press, 1979); Russell F. Weigley, *Quartermaster General of the Union Army: A Biography of M. C. Meigs* (New York: Columbia University Press, 1959); and Erna Risch, *Quartermaster Support of the Army: A History of the Corps, 1775–1939* (Washington: Office of the Quartermaster General, 1962). Contemporary information on clothing and equipment exists in the various editions of *United States Army Regulations* published in 1861, 1863, 1881, and 1889, as well as in the published annual reports of the Secretary of War, 1876–88. The 1876, 1884, and 1885 volumes, moreover, may be of particular interest because of their illustrations. Information on uniforms of the 1870s and 1880s appears in *Uniform of the Army of the United States, 1882* (Philadelphia: Thomas Hunter, 1882), and *Regulations for the Uniform of the Army of the United States with Illustrations* (Philadelphia: Philadelphia Quartermaster Depot, 1888).

Information on specific features of uniforms and insignia of the army during the late nineteenth century appears in the following studies: Sidney B. Brinckerhoff, *Boots and Shoes of the Frontier Soldier* (Tucson: Arizona Historical Society, Museum Monograph No. 7, 1976); Sidney B. Brinckerhoff, *Metal Uniform Insignia of the Frontier U.S. Army, 1846–1902* (Tucson: Arizona Historical Society, Museum Monograph No. 3, 1972); Gordon Chappell, *Brass Spikes and Horsehair Plumes: A Study of U.S. Army Dress Helmets, 1872–1903* (Tucson: Arizona Pioneers' Historical Society, Museum Monograph No. 4, 1966); Gordon Chappell, *Summer Helmets of the U.S. Army, 1875–1910* (Cheyenne: Wyoming State Archives and Historical Department, Museum Monograph No. 1, 1967); Gordon Chappell, *The Search for the Well-Dressed Soldier, 1865–1890* (Tucson: Arizona Historical Society, Museum Monograph No. 5, 1972); William K. Emerson, *Chevrons: Illustrated History and Catalog of U.S. Army Insignia* (Washington: Smithsonian Institution Press, 1983); Edgar M. Howell, *United States Army Headgear, 1855–1902* (Washington: Smithsonian Institution Press, 1975); John Phillip Langellier, "Chevrons of the United States Army, 1861–1897," *American Military Tradition* 1, no. 1 (n.p., n.d.); John Phillip Langellier, *They Continually Wear the Blue: U.S. Army Enlisted Dress Uniforms, 1865–1902* (San Francisco: Barnes-McGee Historical Military Publications, 1974); John Phillip Langellier, "Uniforms of the Seacoast Soldier, 1851–1902," *American Military Tradition* 1, no. 2 (n.p., n.d.); Randy Steffen, *The Horse Soldier, 1776–1943*, 4 vols. (Norman: University of Oklahoma Press, 1978), vols 2 and 3. Data on uniform clothing and equipment can also be found in issues of *Military Collector and Historian: Journal of the Company of Military Historians*. Garrison equipage, particularly that relevant to the barracks environment, is treated in David A. Clary, *These Relics of Barbarism: A History of Furniture in Barracks and Guardhouses of the United States Army, 1800–1880* (Harpers Ferry, W. Va.: National Park Service, 1985).

SPECIFICATIONS

FOR

CLOTHING,

Camp and Garrison Equipage,

AND

Clothing and Equipage Materials.

WITH ILLUSTRATIONS.

PUBLISHED BY DIRECTION OF THE

QUARTERMASTER GENERAL OF THE ARMY,

AT THE

Philadelphia Depot of the Quartermaster's Department.

1889.

WAR DEPARTMENT,

QUARTERMASTER GENERAL'S OFFICE.

Specifications for Cork Helmets.

Shape and weight.—To be in shape according to standard sample, and to weigh about seven and one-fourth ($7\frac{1}{4}$) ounces when finished ; reasonable variations (from this weight) due to sizes to be allowed.

Material, etc.—The shell to be composed of two thicknesses of the best quality of cork, laminated or scarf-seamed, and securely cemented together with shellac. The linings to be firmly shellaced to the inside of shell ; that for the dome to be of slate-colored drilling, and that for the visor or shade to be of emerald-green merino or cashmere. Sweat-leather to be on frame or hoop as in sample, well separated from the shell (for ventilation) by ten (10) small cork studs securely fastened ; sweat to be about one and three-eights ($1\frac{3}{8}$) inch deep, and to be provided with a drawing string. Outside covering to be of the best quality of bleached cotton drilling, in four (4) sections, welt seamed and secured to the shell with shellac. Band of same material, about three-fourths ($\frac{3}{4}$) of an inch deep. Edge to be bound with stout bleached stay-binding. Adjustible ventilator at top as in sample. Chin-strap of white enameled leather, and brass hooks for same, as in sample.

Adopted by the Secretary of War May 5, 1880.

M. C. MEIGS,
Quartermaster General,
Bvt. Major General, U. S. A.

715, F, 1880.

CORK HELMET.

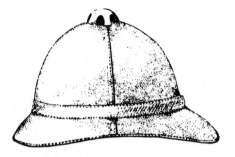

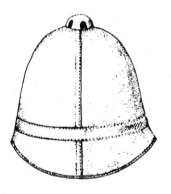

WAR DEPARTMENT,

QUARTERMASTER GENERAL'S OFFICE.

Specifications for Muskrat Caps.

To be made according to standard sample, of muskrat skin, with ear-flaps, cape, and visor, according to pattern. Lining of brown chintz or silesia, padded with cotton wadding.

Sizes same as for dress and forage caps.

Adopted March 12, 1879.

M. C. MEIGS,
Quartermaster General,
Bvt. Major General, U. S. A

337—Q. M. G. O., 1879, Cl. and Eq. supply.

MUSKRAT FUR CAP.

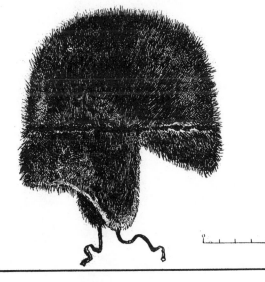

WAR DEPARTMENT,

QUARTERMASTER GENERAL'S OFFICE,

Specifications for Stable Frocks.

Material.—Light canvas or unbleached drilling, equal in quality to that of the standard sample. Metal (trowsers) buttons.

Pattern and dimensions.—To be in shape of a loose sack coat, single breasted, with three (3) buttons, and a standing collar from two (2) to three (3) inches high, according to size. Measures for the four (4) sizes to be as follows:

	Breast measure.	Length.	Collar measure.	Length of sleeve.
	Inches.	*Inches.*	*Inches.*	*Inches.*
Size 1 . .	38	33	17	33
Size 2 . .	39	34	18	33½
Size 3 . .	40	35	19	34
Size 4 . .	42	36	20	34¼

Adopted March 12, 1879.

M. C. MEIGS,
Quartermaster General,
Bvt. Major General, U. S. A.

337—Q. M. G. O., Cl. and Eq. supply.

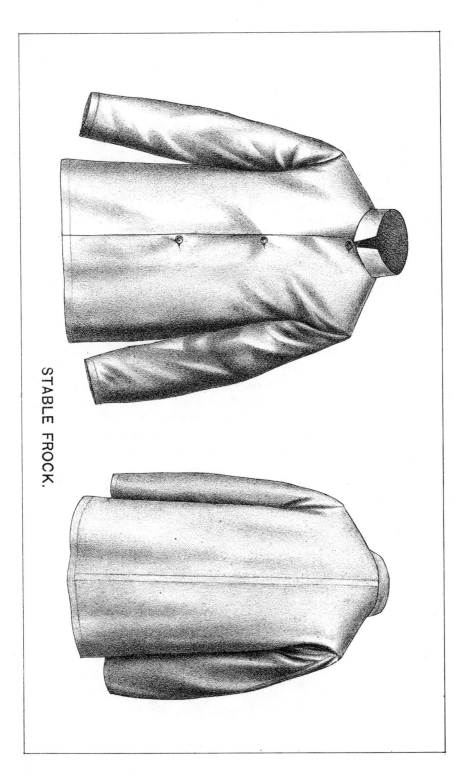

STABLE FROCK.

Specifications for Woolen Stockings.

Wool.—To be about one-half (½) each of good super pulled wool and fine medium or X fleece wool, and to be mixed in the proportion of forty to fifty (40 to 50) per cent. of black and fifty to sixty (50 to 60) per cent. of white, according to the shade required.

Yarn.—To be spun three and a half (3½) run, with eighteen to twenty (18 to 20) holes of twist.

Legs.—To be knit two-thread on a regular two and one (2 and 1) ribbed "Aiken" twelve (12) gauge machine.

Heels.—To be knit four-thread eighteen (18) ribs wide, about three (3) inches long, plain on bottom, and four (4) narrowings. In joining the heel to the foot every stitch must be taken up singly.

Toes.—To be knit four-thread, of white yarn of corresponding quality to the other, and to be regular narrowed.

Tops of Legs.—To be fastened or bound off twice around.

The stockings to be well fulled and shaped, and when finished to weigh three (3) pounds to the dozen pairs.

The legs to be not less than fourteen (14) inches long; the feet to be of three (3) sizes, viz.: 9½, 10½, and 11½ inches, and to be assorted in the following proportion of sizes to the dozen: 5, 9½, 4, 10½, 3, 11½. Size to be plainly stamped on the toe of each stocking.

Adopted June 4, 1877.

M. C. MEIGS,
Quartermaster General,
Bvt. Major General, U. S. A.

549—F—1877.

WOOLEN STOCKING.

WAR DEPARTMENT,
QUARTERMASTER GENERAL'S OFFICE.

Specifications for White Gloves.

Made of strong white cotton known commercially as "Berlin cotton wool." Gored between the fingers. Three (3) welts stitched along the back of hand.

A white elastic band, one-fourth (¼) inch wide, about one (1) inch long, fastened to the inner side of the wrist.

Stitched hem around the wrist. To be of three sizes: No. 9, 10, and 11.

Adopted May 31, 1876.

M. C. MEIGS,
Quartermaster General,
Bvt. Major General, U. S. A.

WHITE BERLIN GLOVES.

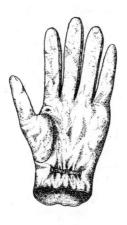

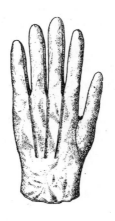

Specifications for Iron Bunks. (*Composite.*)

To consist of two trestles, one for the head, the other for the foot, made of the best quality American wrought-iron, and painted.

Each trestle to have four (4) legs, two on each side, made of wrought-iron bars, one and one-fourth (1¼) inch wide, three-eighths (⅜) of an inch thick, and one (1) foot long, slightly turned up on the bottom.

The two legs on the same side are, at the top, firmly united in a solid iron socket two and one-half (2½) inches long, one and three-fourths (1¾) inch broad, one and one-half (1½) inch high, diverging at right angles with the body of the trestle toward the bottom to a distance of from ten (10) to twelve (12) inches.

The same sockets hold also the cross-piece, an iron bar one and one-fourth (1¼) inch wide, one-half (½) inch thick, and two (2) feet two (2) inches long in the clear. Strongly riveted to this cross-piece are four upright iron pins one-half (½) inch thick and about one and one-half (1½) inch high, at equal distances from each other, to receive and hold the slats. The two outer pins have screw-threads with corresponding thumb-nuts for the better security of the slats. On the top of the socket that connects the cross piece with the legs is another socket, octagonal, two and one-half (2½) inches high and two (2) inches in diameter, to hold the upper frame ; the latter, consisting of two (2) upright iron rods five-eighths (⅝) of an inch thick and about seventeen (17) inches high, an iron rod one-half (½) inch thick across the top of the two uprights, and four iron braces, one-half (½) inch rods, running diagonally from the four corners of the upper frame and meeting at center in an ornamented iron shield with the letters U. S. A.

The two braces running from the upper corners down toward the center are straight ; the lower ones are bent thus— ⌒⌣ ⌣⌐. All the rods forming the upper frame are connected with neatly-turned iron sockets. There are to each bunk four slats, made of pine, ash, oak, or maple wood, about six (6) feet ten (10) inches long, six (6) inches wide, the two outside ones one (1) inch, and the two inside ones three-quarters (¾) of an inch thick. At a distance of one and three-quarters (1¾) inch from each end of the slats are holes of sufficient diameter to admit the slat-pins.

Adopted May 31, 1876.

M. C. MEIGS,
Quartermaster General,
Bvt. Major General, U. S. A.

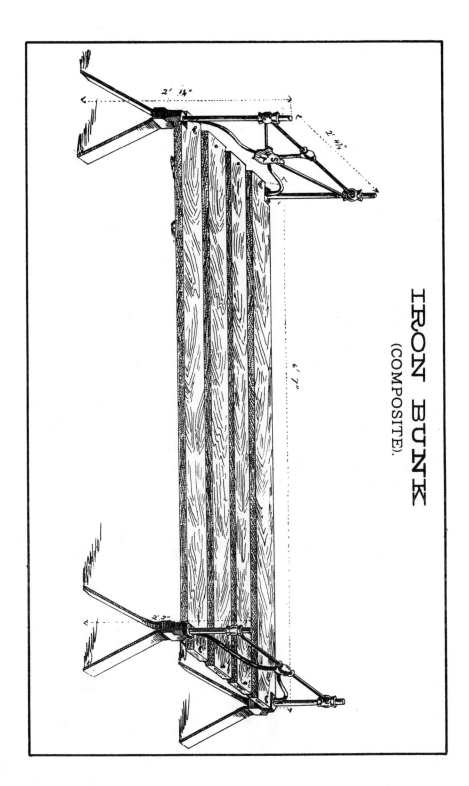

IRON BUNK
(COMPOSITE).

WAR DEPARTMENT,

QUARTERMASTER GENERAL'S OFFICE.

Specifications for Bed Sacks.

Material.—To be made of cotton or linen drilling, or seven (7) ounce cotton duck of good quality.

Size.—Length, six (6) feet ten (10) inches; width, thirty-one and one-quarter (31¼) inches (measurements from corner to corner when filled); depth, four and one-half (4½) inches.

Opening.—To have an opening or fly in the center nineteen (19) inches in length, with one (1) by one and a quarter (1¼) inch stay-piece at each end; opening fastened with four (4) strings of three-quarter (¾) inch tape, placed equidistant from each end.

Finish.—All seams to be double; ends cut square; openings button-hole stitched at each end.

Adopted March 12, 1879.

M. C. MEIGS,
Quartermaster General,
Bvt. Major General, U. S. A.

337—O. M. G. O., 1879, Cl. and Eq. supply.

BED SACK.

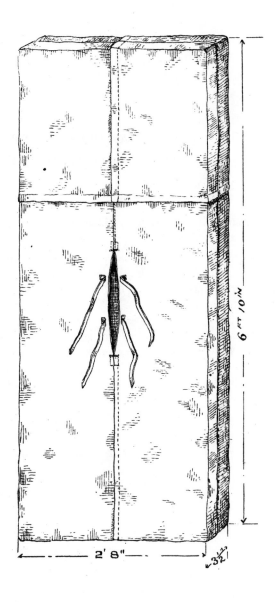

6 FT 10 IN

2' 8"

3½"

o 3 6 9 12

15

WAR DEPARTMENT,

QUARTERMASTER GENERAL'S OFFICE.

Specifications for Pillow Sacks.

Material.—To be made of cotton or linen drilling, or seven (7) ounce cotton duck of good quality.

Dimensions.—Length, when filled, twenty-seven and one-half (27½) inches; width, when filled, seventeen (17) inches; depth, when filled, three and three-fourths (3¾) to four (4) inches. Measurements to be made from corner to corner.

To have an opening or fly in the seam in the upper side seven (7) inches long, to be fastened with two (2) strings of three-quarter (¾) inch cotton tape. Ends of opening to be properly stayed with button-hole stitch.

Ends of sack to be cut square.

Adopted March 12, 1879.

M. C. MEIGS,
Quartermaster General,
Bvt. Major General, U. S. A.

337—Q. M. G. O., 1879, Cl. and Eq. supply.

PILLOW SACK.

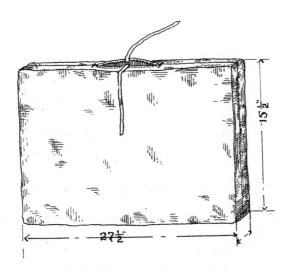

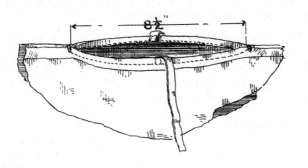

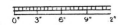

WAR DEPARTMENT,

QUARTERMASTER GENERAL'S OFFICE.

Specifications for Trumpets.

For all Foot Troops.—To be the same as standard sample Brass Trumpet "F," two (2) coil, and with two (2) mouth pieces. When complete, with mouth-piece in, to weigh about twelve and a half (12½) ounces, and to measure about sixteen (16) inches in length, and about four and a half (4½) inches in width at center. Diameter of bell to be about four and a half inches.

For all Mounted Troops.—To be the "F" Trumpet, as described above, with the addition of a detachable "C" crook. The crook to weigh about three and a half (3½) ounces, and to occupy a space, as bent, of about ten (10) by three and a half (3½) inches. Length complete, about nineteen (19) inches.

Adopted February 15, 1879.

M. C. MEIGS,
Quartermaster General,
Bvt. Major General, U. S. A.

TRUMPETS.

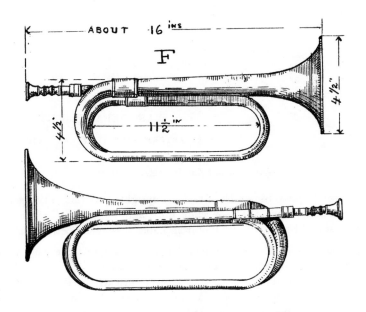

ABOUT 16 ins

F

4½"

11½ in

4½"

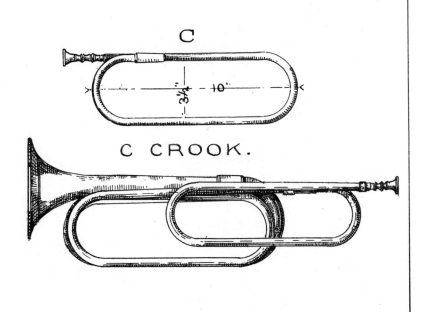

C

3¼" 10"

C CROOK.

WAR DEPARTMENT,
QUARTERMASTER GENERAL'S OFFICE.

Specifications for Hospital Tent Poles.

A set of poles to consist of two (2) uprights and one (1) ridge, the former to be made of ash or white pine, and the latter of white pine, clear straight-grained, and free from knots or other imperfections.

Dimensions.—Ridge, fourteen (14) feet long, three and three-quarter ($3\frac{3}{4}$) inches wide, two and three-quarter ($2\frac{3}{4}$) inches thick; on each end a band, four (4) inches wide, of galvanized iron, secured by ten (10) copper nails. A three-quarter ($\frac{3}{4}$) inch hole bored through at a distance of two and a quarter ($2\frac{1}{4}$) inches from each end, for the spindle of uprights.

The uprights octagonal, twelve (12) feet long and three (3) inches thick. Band of galvanized iron three and one-fourth ($3\frac{1}{4}$) inches wide on upper ends, secured by four (4) one (1) inch screws. Spindle of five-eighths ($\frac{5}{8}$) inch round iron, galvanized, driven three (3) inches into upper end and projecting six (6) inches.

Adopted March 12, 1879.

M. C. MEIGS,
Quartermaster General,
Bvt. Major General, U. S. A.

337—Q. M. G. O., 1879, Cl. and Eq. supply.

TENT POLES.

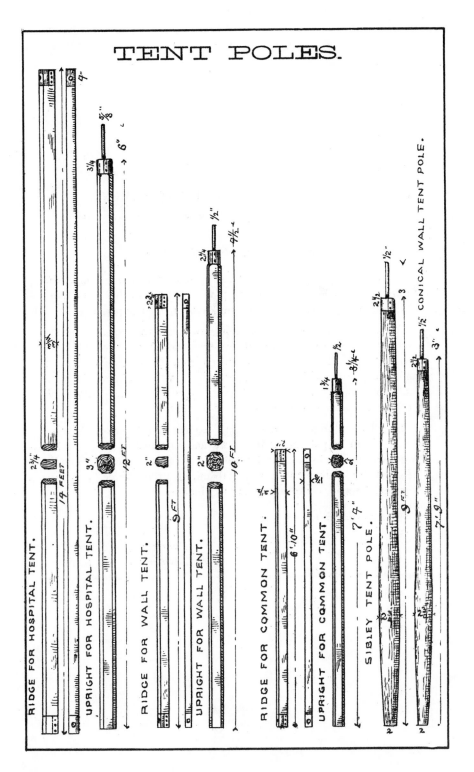

Specifications for Wall-Tent Poles.

A set of poles to consist of two (2) uprights and one (1) ridge, the former to be made of ash or white pine, and the latter of white pine, clear, straight-grained, and free from knots or other imperfections.

Ridge.—Ridge nine (9) feet long, two and three-quarters (2¾) inches wide, two (2) inches thick ; on each end a band, two and three-quarter (2¾) inches wide, of galvanized iron, secured by four (4) one and one-quarter (1¼) inch copper nails. A five-eighths (⅝) of an inch hole bored through at a distance of one and one-quarter inch (1¼) from each end for the spindle of uprights.

Uprights.—Uprights octagonal, ten (10) feet long and two (2) inches thick ; band of galvanized iron, two and one-quarter (2¼) inches wide, on upper ends, secured by two (2) one (1) inch screws. Spindle of one-half (½) inch round iron, galvanized, driven three (3) inches into upper ends and projecting four (4) inches.

Adopted March 12, 1879.

M. C. MEIGS,
Quartermaster General,
Bvt. Major General, U. S. A.

337—Q. M. G. O., 1879, Cl. and Eq. supply.

WAR DEPARTMENT,

QUARTERMASTER GENERAL'S OFFICE.

Specifications for Shelter Tent Poles

A set of shelter tent poles, to consist of two (2) uprights, round, one (1) inch in diameter and three (3) feet ten (10) inches long, to be made of poplar, pine, or other suitable wood. Each upright to be in two (2) parts, of about equal length, beveled and joined in a tin socket four (4) inches long, firmly soldered and secured to lower part with two (2) tacks. A shoulder, three-quarters ($\frac{3}{4}$) of an inch deep, to be turned on upper end of uprights, making a spindle or stud one-half ($\frac{1}{2}$) of an inch in diameter.

Adopted March 12, 1879.

M. C. MEIGS,
Quartermaster General,
Bvt. Major General, U. S. A.

337—Q. M. G. O., 1879, Cl. and Eq. supply.

WAR DEPARTMENT,

QUARTERMASTER GENERAL'S OFFICE.

Specifications for Garrison Flags.

To be made of bunting, thirty-six (36) feet fly and twenty (20) feet hoist; thirteen (13) horizontal stripes of equal breadth, alternately red and white, beginning with the red. In the upper quarter, next the staff, is the "Union," composed of a number of white stars equal to the number of States in the Union, (each star measuring ten (10) inches between the farthest point, arranged in five (5) rows parallel to the longer edges of the flag,) on a blue field, one-third (⅓) the length of the flag, and extending to the lower edge of the fourth red stripe from the top. The heading to be of stout eight (8) ounce cotton duck, seven (7) inches wide, doubled to the flag, making it three and one-half (3½) inches wide when completed, and having a piece of stout two (2) inch webbing through it extending the whole width of the flag.

To have on each corner of flag at heading a triangular stay-piece of bunting, the horizontal side of which is twelve (12) inches, the vertical side ten (10) inches.

A galvanized iron staple and ring ( ) at each end of flag-heading, fastened with five (5) copper rivets.

The lower edge or bottom of fly to be turned in three (3) thicknesses, with three (3) rows of sewing on it to strengthen the flag.

Adopted May 31, 1876.

M. C. MEIGS,
Quartermaster General,
Bvt. Major General, U. S A.

GARRISON FLAG.

WAR DEPARTMENT,
QUARTERMASTER GENERAL'S OFFICE.

Specifications for Post-Flags.

The same as garrison-flags in every respect, all the parts being proportionately smaller, and to be of the following dimensions, viz: twenty (20) feet fly and ten (10) feet hoist, stars six (6) inches between farthest points, stay-pieces eight (8) by ten (10) inches, and heading three (3) inches wide when completed.

Adopted May 31, 1876.

M. C. MEIGS,
Quartermaster General,
Bvt. Major General, U. S. A.

POST FLAG.

Specifications for Storm and Recruiting Flags.

The dimensions of the flag to be eight (8) feet fly, and four (4) feet two (2) inches hoist. To be made of bunting, and to have thirteen (13) horizontal stripes of equal width, alternately red and white, beginning with the red. The "Union," in the upper quarter next the head, to consist of a blue field, displaying a number of white stars equal to the number of States in the Union, arranged in five (5) rows, parallel to the stripes. Size of stars three and one-quarter (3¼) inches between the opposite points.

Size of the "Union" one-third (⅓) the length of the flag, and to extend to the lower edge of the fourth red stripe from top.

The heading to be of stout eight (8) ounce cotton duck, four (4) inches wide, doubled to the flag, making it two (2) inches wide when completed, and to have a piece of stout one and a half (1½) inch webbing through it, extending the whole width of the flag.

A galvanized iron staple and ring at each end of the flag heading, fastened with three (3) copper rivets.

To have on each corner of the flag, at heading, a triangular stay-piece of bunting, the horizontal side of which shall be seven (7) inches, and the vertical side five (5) inches.

The lower edge or bottom of fly to be turned in three (3) thicknesses, with three (3) rows of sewing on it to strengthen the flag.

Adopted December 31, 1877.

STEWART VAN VLIET,
Acting Quartermaster General,
Bvt. Major General, U. S. A.

FLAG

STORM AND RECRUITING.

WAR DEPARTMENT,
QUARTERMASTER GENERAL'S OFFICE.

Specifications for Flag-Halliards.

For garrison and storm flags: To be made of the best American or Italian hemp, composed of four strands, each three folds, hard twisted, two hundred and twenty (220) feet long, three-eighths ($\frac{3}{8}$) of an inch in diameter, and to weigh eleven (11) pounds each.

For recruiting flags: Of the same material, of four strands, with two folds each, hard twisted, forty-seven (47) feet long, three-sixteenths ($\frac{3}{16}$) of an inch in diameter, and to weigh nine (9) pounds to the dozen.

Adopted May 31, 1876.

M. C. MEIGS,
Quartermaster General,
Bvt. Major General, U. S. A.

FLAG HALLIARD
WITH DEVICES.

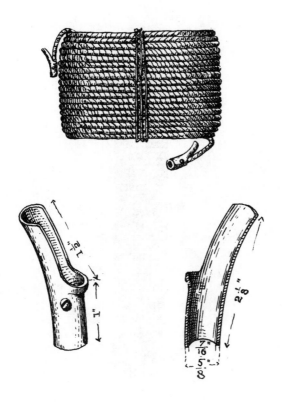

FLAG HALLIARD.

WAR DEPARTMENT,

QUARTERMASTER GENERAL'S OFFICE.

Specifications for Stencil-Plates.

A complete set of stencil-plates consists of two full alphabets, Roman capitals, and including the usual mark for " &," and two series of numbers from " 1 to 0."

One set of letters and numbers to be one (1) inch, the other one-half (½) inch high. They are cut on plates of sheet-brass, No. 28, the larger two and a quarter (2¼) by two (2) inches, the smaller one and three-quarters (1¾) by one and a half (1½) inch. The upper edge of each plate is turned up so as to form a rim about one-half (½) inch high.

These plates are issued in Japanned tin boxes eight and a half (8½) inches long, four (4) inches wide, and one and three-quarters (1¾) inch high, with hinged lids. Each box contains, besides the full set of stencils, a cake of marking-paste in tin box, a sponge, and a stencil-brush. Printed directions for thê use of the latter materials are fastened to the inside of the lid.

Adopted May 31, 1876.

M. C. MEIGS,
Quartermaster General,
Bvt. Major General, U. S. A.

STENCIL PLATES.

5¼"

WAR DEPARTMENT,
QUARTERMASTER GENERAL'S OFFICE.

Specifications for Canton Flannel.

To be made of long-staple American cotton, free from dirt or imperfections, and of a grade not inferior to that known commercially as "low middling." To be thirty (30) inches wide, and nap raised. To weigh six (6) ounces to the linear yard; to contain not less than seventy (70) threads of warp and fifty (50) threads of filling to the inch, and to be capable of sustaining a strain, to the inch (tested in the piece), of sixty (60) pounds on the warp and fifty (50) pounds on the filling. The flannel to be unbleached.

Approved July 24, 1877.

M. C. MEIGS,
Quartermaster General,
Bvt. Major General, U. S. A.

728, F, 1877.

36

WAR DEPARTMENT,

QUARTERMASTER GENERAL'S OFFICE.

Specifications for Twelve-ounce Cotton Duck.

To be made of American cotton, of a grade not inferior to "low middling," and woven in a workmanlike manner, free from imperfections. To be full twenty-eight and one-half (28½) inches wide when finished, and to weigh not less than twelve (12) ounces to the linear yard. To contain not less than forty-four (44) threads of warp, nor less than thirty (30) threads of filling to the inch, and to be capable of sustaining a strain of not less than one hundred and twenty-eight (128) pounds in the warp and eighty-four (84) pounds in the filling to the half (½) inch, tested in the piece. To be entirely free from sizing, and not to be "hot finished."

Adopted March 12, 1879, in lieu of those adopted February 25, 1875.

M. C. MEIGS,
Quartermaster General,
Bvt. Major General, U. S. A.

337—Q. M. G. O., 1879, Cl. and Eq. Supply.

37

WAR DEPARTMENT,

QUARTERMASTER GENERAL'S OFFICE.

Specifications for Ten-ounce Cotton Duck.

To be made of American cotton, of a grade not inferior to "low middling," and woven in a workmanlike manner, free from imperfections. To be full twenty-eight and one-half (28½) inches wide when finished, and to weigh not less than ten (10) ounces to the linear yard. To contain not less than forty-six (46) threads of warp, nor less than thirty-two (32) threads of filling to the inch, and to be capable of sustaining a strain of not less than one hundred and eight (108) pounds in the warp and sixty-four (64) pounds in the filling to the half (½) inch, tested in the piece. To be entirely free from sizing, and not to be "hot finished."

Adopted March 12, 1879.

M. C. MEIGS,
Quartermaster General,
Bvt. Major General, U. S. A.

337.—Q. M. G. O., 1879, Cl. and Eq. supply.

WAR DEPARTMENT,

QUARTERMASTER GENERAL'S OFFICE.

Specifications for Eight-ounce Cotton Duck.

To be made of American cotton, of a grade not inferior to "low middling," and woven in a workmanlike manner, free from imperfections. To be full twenty-eight and one-half (28½) inches wide when finished, and to weigh not less than eight (8) ounces to the linear yard. To contain not less than fifty (50) threads of warp, nor less than thirty-two (32) threads of filling to the inch, and to be capable of sustaining a strain of not less than seventy-eight (78) pounds in the warp and forty-five (45) pounds in the filling to the half (½) inch, tested in the piece. To be entirely free from sizing and not to be "hot finished."

Adopted March 12, 1879.

M. C. MEIGS,
Quartermaster General,
Bvt. Major General, U. S. A.

337—Q. M. G, O., 1879, Cl. and Eq. supply.

WAR DEPARTMENT,

QUARTERMASTER GENERAL'S OFFICE.

Specifications for Sibley or Conical Wall Tent Stoves.

Stove.—The stove to be in the form of the frustum of a cone, and to be made of No. 15 (American gauge) common annealed plate iron. To be in one piece, (except the collar and door) and the seam at back to be fastened with twenty-four (24) rivets. The collar at top to be of the same material as the stove. To be two and a half (2½) inches deep, and be secured to the stove by six (6) rivets. Aperture for door to be about six (6) inches high by six (6) inches wide, the upper corners of which shall be rounded as in sample. The door to be sufficiently large to lap over the aperture; to be securely hinged to the stove, and to be properly molded to its form. An "A"-shaped vent at the bottom of stove directly under the door, about two (2) inches high by three (3) inches wide; the top to be rounded.

Dimension and weight.—Height to top of collar, twenty-eight (28) inches. Circumference (outside) at bottom, fifty-eight (58) inches; at top, thirteen (13) inches. Distance from bottom of door aperture to base of stove, fourteen (14) inches. Weight about nineteen (19) pounds, (to average not less than this).

Adopted December 3, 1880.

M. C. MEIGS,
Quartermaster General,
Bvt. Major General, U. S. A.

1713—Q. M. G. O., 1880. C. & Eq. Supplies.

STOVE.

FOR SIBLEY & CONICAL WALL TENT.

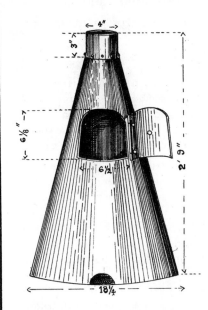
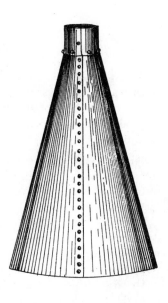

WAR DEPARTMENT,

QUARTERMASTER GENERAL'S OFFICE.

Specifications for Undershirts.

Material.—The mixture to consist of fifty per centum ($50^o/_o$) of super-pulled natural sheeps-grey and fine medium or $\times$ fleece wool, mixed to the shade of standard sample, and fifty per centum ($50^o/_o$) of good middling cotton, and to be free from shoddy, flocks, reworked wool or other impurities.   The whole mixture to be thoroughly carded.

Workmanship.—To be *firmly knit* on a sixteen (16) gauge machine; to be "taken up" on the shoulder, self-finish with "regular" cuffs; to be bound with drab Prussian binding around the neck and down the breast opening.

To have three (3) eighteen (18) line pearl buttons on front, and corresponding buttonholes properly made; to be scoured in the garment, and dried on forms   To be finished like, and equal in all respects to, the standard sample.

To be six (6) sizes, the breast measures and lengths of which shall be as described, and the weights not less than the figures given below:

Size Numbers . .	1	2	3	4	5	6
Breast Measure .	36 ins.	38 ins.	40 ins.	42 ins.	44 ins.	46 ins.
Length of Shirt .	31 ins.	32 ins.	33 ins.	34 ins.	34 ins.	35 ins.
Weight	14 ozs.	15½ ozs.	16½ ozs.	18 ozs.	19 ozs.	20 ozs.

To be manufactured in the following proportion of sizes to the one hundred : $\frac{5}{1} \frac{25}{2} \frac{35}{3} \frac{20}{4} \frac{10}{5} \frac{5}{6} = 100$.

Adopted February 16, 1881.

M. C. MEIGS,
Quartermaster General,
Bvt. Major General U. S. A.

246—Q. M. G. O., 1881.   C. & Eq. Supplies.

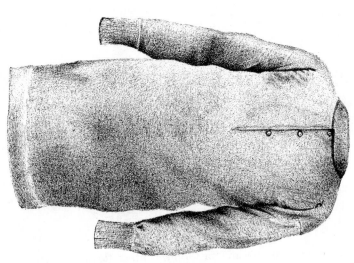

UNDERSHIRT.

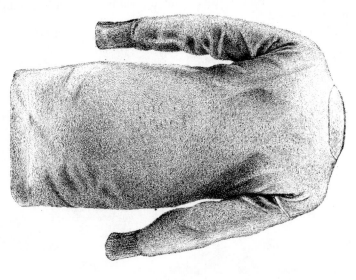

WAR DEPARTMENT,

QUARTERMASTER GENERAL'S OFFICE.

Specifications for Card Receivers.

To be made of tin, and in form according to the standard sample. The upper front and edges to be japanned emerald green. Height at center about three and five-eights ($3\frac{5}{8}$) inches, width about three and three-fourths ($3\frac{3}{4}$) inches. The edge at sides and bottom to be turned over front about one-eighth ($\frac{1}{8}$) of an inch full, leaving sufficient room to allow the sliding of an ordinary bristol-board card. Height of turned-over edges at sides about two and three-fourths ($2\frac{3}{4}$) inches. A round hole three-sixteenths ($\frac{3}{16}$) of an inch in diameter in the upper edge at center.

To be fully equal to the standard sample in quality and finish.

Adopted February 20, 1882.

D. H. RUCKER,
Quartermaster General, U. S. A.

CARD RECEIVER.

WAR DEPARTMENT,
QUARTERMASTER GENERAL'S OFFICE.

Specifications for Scrubbing-brushes.

The block to be made of oak, ten (10) inches long, one-half (½) inch thick, one (1) end miter-shaped.

The tail or straight end of the block, on the mitred edge, to have two (2) parallel rows of six (6) and seven (7) knots, respectively, one (1) inch long, slanting outward; the curved front end of the block, on the mitred edge, to have one (1) row of thirteen (13) knots, one (1) inch long, slanting outward.

The body of the brush is to be five (5) inches long, and to contain four (4) rows of eleven (11) knots each, and three (3) rows of twelve (12) knots each, cut three-fourths (¾) of an inch high from the wood.

The peak to be three (3) inches long, and to contain forty (40) knots, cut seven-eighths (⅞) of an inch high above the wood. There are to be altogether one hundred and fifty (150) knots, drawn through the block with good, strong wire fastenings. Knots to be made of the best sharp, strong western bristles.

The back of the block must be covered with bass-wood, or other suitable wood, one-eighth (⅛) of an inch thick, firmly nailed to it.

Adopted September 29, 1882, in lieu of specifications adopted May 31, 1876, which are hereby canceled.

RUFUS INGALLS,
Quartermaster General,
Bvt. Major General, U. S. A.

1038 Q. M. G. O., 1882—C. & Eq., suppl.

SCRUBBING BRUSH.

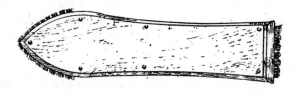

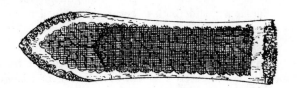

Specifications for Drum-Slings.

To be made of heavy two and one-eighth (2⅛) inch cotton cadet web, in *two pieces*, thirty-eight (38) and ten (10) inches long in the clear, held together by a leather frog, pear-shaped, three and five-eighths (3⅝) inches long, two and five-eighths (2⅝) inches wide at the broadest, and one and a half (1½) at the lowest part. The webbing to be let into the frog in such way that the long part passes under the left arm and over the right shoulder, the short part over the right breast of wearer, and at such angle that, when worn, it hangs perfectly smooth.

AN OBLONG TONGUELESS BUCKLE, two and five-eights (2⅝) inches by one and a quarter (1¼) inch, of strong brass, five sixteenths ($\frac{5}{16}$) of an inch wide, with catch on inner side at the end of shorter part, and a slide of the same material seven sixteenths ($\frac{7}{16}$) of an inch wide at the end of longer part, for the purpose of lengthening or shortening the sling. Buckle and slide both to be neatly fastened to webbing by three (3) rivets each.

A TRIANGLE of one-eighth (⅛) inch brass wire, to receive hook of drum at the lower end of frog, to which it is fastened by a leather loop let into the frog and securely stitched. Each side of triangle to be one (1) inch long.

Adopted January 15, 1883.

RUFUS INGALLS,
Quartermaster General,
Bvt. Major General, U. S. A.

1711—Q. M. G. O., 1882, C. and Eq. supply.

DRUM SLING.

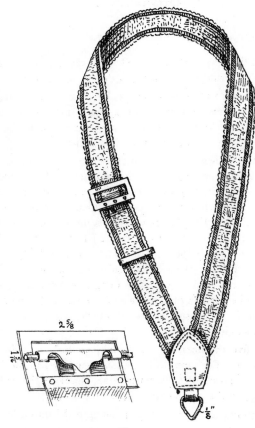

BUCKLE

2 ⅝
2 ½

⅛"

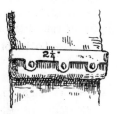

2 ½"

SLIDE.

WAR DEPARTMENT,

QUARTERMASTER GENERAL'S OFFICE.

Specifications for Cotton Stockings.

Colors.—To be of three (3) colors, viz : Gray mixed, Brown mixed, and White (unbleached), and to be put up in dozens of one color.

Material.—The brown and gray mixed to be of good long-staple American cotton, free from impurities, of a grade not lower than "New Orleans middling," double carded ; and the white to be of good long-staple American cotton, free from impurities.

Workmanship.—The brown and gray mixed to be "full regular," made according to the standard sample, with fashioned heels and toes ; the yarn to be spun from two (2) rovings in the regular hosiery twist for cotton. The top to be ribbed to a depth of about four and a half (4½) inches and to be joined to the leg without seam or linking, forming an integral part of the stocking ; to be knitted from three (3) No. 14 yarns and have the upper edge welted. The leg and foot to be knitted of three (3) No. 13 yarns. The substance of heel to be increased by an additional yarn of No. 25. Length of leg from lower edge of ribbed top to be not less than seven and one-half (7½) inches. The white (unbleached) to be similar to the above, except that the yarn be spun from a single roving.

Sizes.—To be of five (5) sizes, viz: 9½-inch, 10-inch, 10½-inch, 11-inch, and 11½-inch. Each size to be put up separate, in the following proportions : sixteen 9½, thirty-two 10, twenty-eight 10½, sixteen 11, eight 11½ to the one hundred pairs.

Weight.—To weigh not less than two (2) pounds to the dozen pairs.

Adopted February 23, 1883, in lieu of specifications adopted March 12, 1879, (No. 22,) which are hereby canceled.

RUFUS INGALLS,
Quartermaster General,
Bvt. Major General, U. S. A.

470—Q. M. G. O., 1883, C. and Eq. Suppl.

50

COTTON STOCKING.

WAR DEPARTMENT,

QUARTERMASTER GENERAL'S OFFICE.

Specifications for Dark-Blue Indigo Coat Cloth.

To be fifty-four (54) inches, or $\frac{6}{4}$ wide, and to be made of pure American fleece wool, not less than three-quarter to full blood, free from shoddy, flocks, or other impurities. To be twilled, and to be finished to the standard sample.

To contain not less than sixty-six (66) threads of warp and sixty (60) threads of filling in each square inch. To weigh not less than twenty (20) ounces to the linear yard. To be capable of sustaining a strain of fifty (50) pounds to the inch in width of warp and forty-two (42) pounds to the inch in width of filling.

The color to be same shade of dark blue as the standard sample, and to be dyed in the wool with pure indigo, and to have a yellow or white woolen list.

Adopted April 4, 1883, in lieu of specifications adopted May 31, 1876, which are hereby canceled.

ALEX. J. PERRY,
Acting Quartermaster General, U. S. A.

711, Q. M. G. O., 1883—C. & Eq. Suppl.

Specifications for Canvas Overcoats, blanket-lined.

Material.—The Overcoats to be made of ten (10) ounce brown cotton duck, lined throughout (body, sleeves, and collar) with heavy blanket cloth.

Shape.—To be double-breasted, frock skirt, slashed at the back to within about eight (8) inches of the waist-belt; pockets on both sides covered with flaps four (4) inches by eight (8) inches, lined with blanket cloth, to be worn either inside or out. Large collar, fastened by a strap (of brown duck) about 5½ inches by 1¾ inches, with button-hole at each end.

Buttons.—The coats to have ten (10) rubber buttons 1⅛ inches in diameter, five on each breast, placed equidistant, starting one inch below the collar seam. The collar to have three (3) rubber buttons ¾-inch in diameter, one on each side, to fasten the collar when turned up, and one to take up the strap of collar when it is turned down.

Loops.—The loops by which the coat is buttoned across the breast to be about six (6) inches long, made of ¼-inch black mohair cord, and secured to the coat under the buttons.

Waist-belt.—To be made of the same material as the body of the coat, three (3) inches wide, to fasten with a japanned-iron buckle or slide, and to be supported on each side of the coat by supporters, made of the same material, placed over the side seams.

SIZES.

	No. 1.	No. 2.	No 3.	No. 4.
	Inches.	*Inches.*	*Inches.*	*Inches.*
Length of coats	50	52	54	56
Breadth of back	9¼	9½	10	10½
Length of sleeve	33	34	35	36
Width of collar	5½	5¾	6	6½
Width of breast	40	42	44	46
Width of waist	36	38	40	42

Adopted October 24, *1883, and conforming to standard sample approved October* 13, *1883.*

.S. B. HOLABIRD,
Quartermaster General, U. S. A.

2135—Q. M. G. O., 1883, C. & Eq. Suppl.

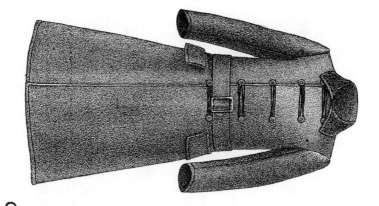

CANVAS OVERCOAT.

BLANKET LINED.

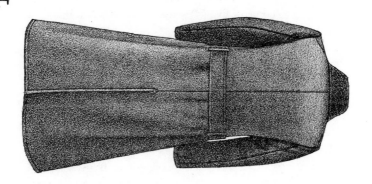

WAR DEPARTMENT,

QUARTERMASTER GENERAL'S OFFICE.

Specifications for Overshirts.

Materials.
Dark-blue wool flannel, Army standard, and hard-rubber buttons, 23 ligne.

Pattern.
To be according to sample, loose, with falling collar (without band), single plait two (2) inches wide on front, and with cuffs. Two (2) outside "patch" breast pockets about seven (7) inches deep by six (6) inches wide, rounded at bottoms. The side seams open about nine (9) inches from bottom, and secured at top of opening with a stay of white-cotton binding well stitched on the inside. Buttons and button holes to be at each of the following places, viz : One (1) at the throat; two (2) on the front plait equidistant between the throat and bottom of opening; one (1) at the centre of the mouth of each pocket, and one (1) on each cuff, making seven (7) in all. Corners of cuffs and bottom of shirt to be rounded off.

Dimensions.
Depth of collar for average size about three (3) inches in front and two and one-quarter ($2\frac{1}{4}$) inches behind; of cuff about two and one-half ($2\frac{1}{2}$) inches; of front plait about fourteen (14) inches.

Sizes.
To be of five (5) sizes, measuring as follows :

	No. 1.	No. 2.	No. 3.	No. 4.	No. 5.
Length of Shirt . . .	33 inches.	33 inches.	34 inches.	35 inches.	36 inches.
Length of Sleeve . .	32½ "	33 "	34 "	35 "	36 "
Collar	15 "	15½ "	16¼ "	17 "	17½ "
Cuff	7½ "	8 "	8½ "	9 "	9½ "

Adopted November 26, 1883, *in lieu of specifications adopted April* 12. 1883, *which are hereby canceled.*

S. B. HOLABIRD,
Quartermaster General, U. S. A.

2349—Q. M. G. O., 1883. C. and Eq. Suppl.

OVERSHIRT.

WAR DEPARTMENT,

QUARTERMASTER GENERAL'S OFFICE.

Specifications for Canvas Sack Coats.

Material.—Six (6) ounce cotton duck, dyed brown.

Pattern.—To be a single-breasted sack coat, with falling collar, and having six (6) india-rubber buttons in front from waist to neck; to have an outside pocket sewed on each breast.

Workmanship.—To be cut and made in accordance with the standard patterns and samples.

SIZES.	Breast Measure.	Waist Measure.	Length of Coat.	Length of Sleeve.	Length of Collar.
	Inches.	*Inches.*	*Inches.*	*Inches.*	*Inches.*
1.	36	34	28	31½	17
2.	37	35	28½	32½	17½
3.	39	37	29	33	18
4.	41	39	29½	34	19
5.	42	40	30½	34¾	20
6.	44	43	31½	35	20¼

Adopted May 31, 1884.

S. B. HOLABIRD,
Quartermaster General, U. S. A.

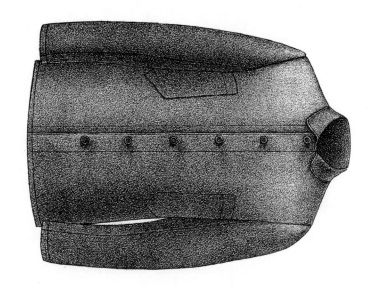

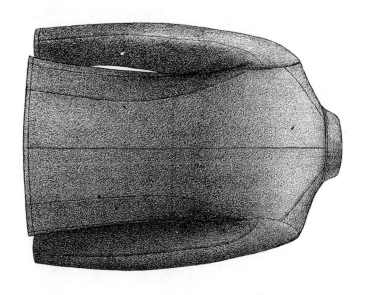

CANVAS SACK COAT.

Specifications for Canvas Trousers.

Material.—Six (6) ounce cotton duck, dyed brown.

Pattern.—To have slanting top pockets, a watch pocket, and a hip pocket on the right side, straps and buckles; waist-band and flies faced with the same material the trousers are made of.

Workmanship.—To be cut and made in accordance with the standard samples.

Sizes.	Waist.	Seat.	Inside Seam.	Outside Seam.	Bottom.
	Inches.	*Inches.*	*Inches.*	*Inches.*	*Inches.*
1	31	36	30½	40½	19½
2	32	38	31	41½	20
3	33	40	32	43½	20½
4	34	42	33	44½	20½
5	36	44	34	45½	21
6	40	45	35	46½	21

Adopted May 31, 1884.

S. B. HOLABIRD,
Quartermaster General, **U. S. A.**

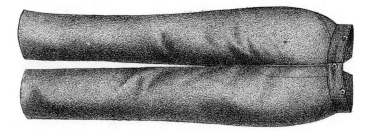

CANVAS TROUSERS.

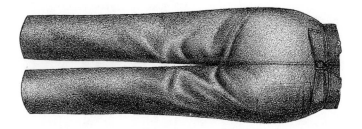

WAR DEPARTMENT,

QUARTERMASTER GENERAL'S OFFICE.

Specifications for Mosquito Bars.

Material.—To be made of the best quality barred mosquito netting and white cotton tape, equal in quality to the same materials in the standard sample.

Dimensions.—Seven (7) feet long, two (2) feet eight (8) inches wide, and five (5) feet eight (8) inches high.

To be bound around top and down the four corners with white tape, and to have two (2) strings of white tape nine (9) inches long, strongly sewed on each of the four upper corners, and to conform in all respects to the standard sample adopted May 23, 1884.

Adopted June 7, 1884.

S. B. HOLABIRD,
Quartermaster General, U. S. A.

1250—F., 1884.

MOSQUITO BAR.

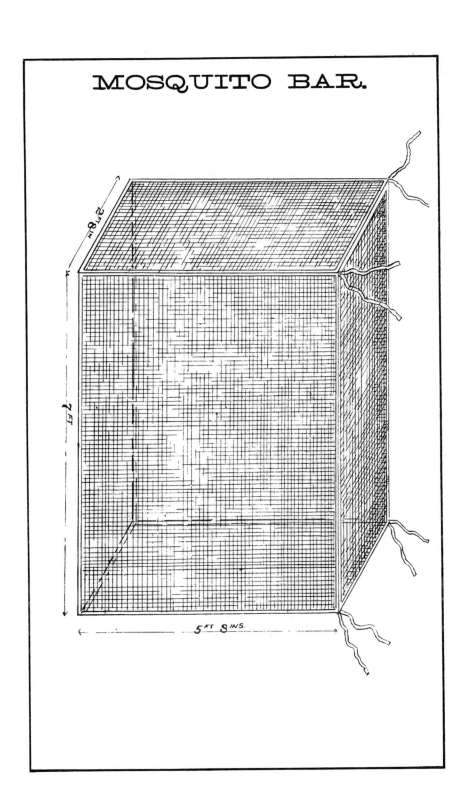

WAR DEPARTMENT,

QUARTERMASTER GENERAL'S OFFICE.

Specifications for Sibley or Conical Wall Tent Stove-pipe.

To be made of best quality refined sheet-iron, No. 24 (American gauge), swaged, grooved, and riveted.

Joints to be twenty-four (24) inches long, and of proper diameter to fit collar of stove, which is thirteen (13) inches outside circumference.

Adopted September 27, 1884, in lieu of specifications of December 3, 1880, which are hereby canceled.

S. B. HOLABIRD,
Quartermaster General, U. S. A.

2242—F., 1884.

STOVE PIPE.

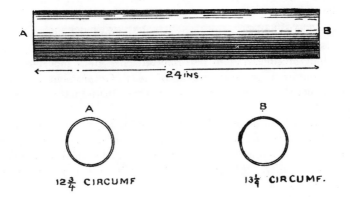

A ———————————————— B

24 INS.

A

12¾ CIRCUMF

B

13¼ CIRCUMF.

WAR DEPARTMENT,

QUARTERMASTER GENERAL'S OFFICE.

Specifications for Color Belt and Sling.

Belt.—To be of best quality of black bridle leather, one and three-fourths (1¾) inches, full, in width, with a girth of forty (40) inches exclusive of clasp fastenings, and to be finished with a cast-brass clasp plate having the letters "U. S." raised in center and a brass outlet buckle.

Sling.—The cylindrical cup to receive the end of the pike to be of cast-brass, one and one-eighth (1⅛) inches in inside diameter, with rim around top edge, and to be firmly attached by a movable ball-socket to a heart-shaped plate of brass of No. 19 Government standard, in the manner shown by sample in office of the Quartermaster General, U. S. A.

The brass plate to be securely fastened by six (6) rivets to a leather base of same shape and of double thickness, and having on its under side a tufted pad covered with pebble leather and stuffed with curled hair of best quality. All of the leathers to be well sewed together around the edge.

Two (2) leather straps one and seven-eighths (1⅞) inches wide and twelve (12) inches long, and two (2) leather straps one and seven-eighths (1⅞) inches wide and fifty-two (52) inches long, to be securely sewed to the upper sides and top of the leather heart-shaped base in the manner shown by sample in the office of the Quartermaster General, U. S. A.

The shorter straps to be finished with a cast-brass buckle having an opening of one and seven-eighths (1⅞) inches wide, and the longer straps to have holes punched in the ends to receive tongue of buckle.

When in use the long strap on the right to be buckled to the short one on the left, and the short strap on the left to the long one on the right.

All leather, except covering of pad, be be of best quality black bridle leather.

Adopted October 9, 1884.

S. B. HOLABIRD,
Quartermaster General, U. S. A.

2369—F., 1884.

COLOR BELT & SLING.

WAR DEPARTMENT,

Quartermaster General's Office.

Specifications for Canvas Mittens.

Material.—The mittens to be made of six (6) oz. cotton duck, dyed brown.

Style.—Plain mitten with thumb only, and having a gauntlet cuff neatly stitched on at the wrist.

Sizes and Workmanship.—Length of mittens from the tip of the hand to the wrist at the point where the cuff is joined : for No. 1, (9) nine inches; for No. 2, (9½) nine and one-half inches; for No. 3, (10) ten inches. Width across the palm of the hand: No. 1, (4¼) four and one-quarter inches; No. 2, (4½) four and one-half inches; No. 3, (5) five inches.

Depth of cuff when finished (4¾) four and three-quarter inches. Length of thumbs from tip to wrist: for No. 1, (4¾) four and three-quarter inches; No. 2, (5) five inches; No. 3, (5½) five and one-half inches; to be neatly and securely stitched on the mitten.

The cuff to be formed and neatly stitched to the mitten, and finished with one-half inch turned in at the edge, and securely and neatly stitched.

The entire mitten to be made in a neat and workmanlike manner, and to conform to the sealed standard samples.

Adopted October 14, 1884.

S. B. HOLABIRD,
Quartermaster General, U. S. A.

2407—F., 1884.

68

CANVAS MITTENS.

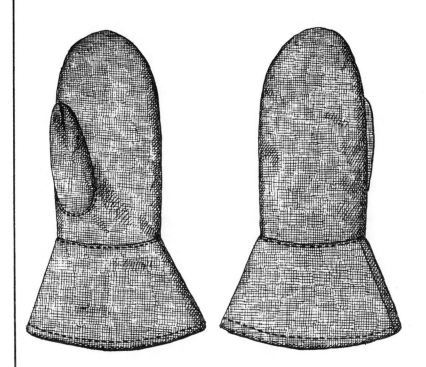

WAR DEPARTMENT,

QUARTERMASTER GENERAL'S OFFICE.

Specifications for Drum-cases.

Material.—Six (6) ounce cotton duck, and white cotton cord (65 fathoms to the pound).

Pattern.—Round bottom case or bag, with drawing strings.

Size.—Bottom sixteen (16) inches in diameter when finished; depth when finished twenty (20) inches; width at the opening thirty (30) inches.

Workmanship.—Bottom flat stitched, with two (2) rows of stitching three-eighths (⅜) inch apart; one (1) inch hem at the opening, with worked holes on each side for the drawing strings, which are arranged to pull both ways, closing the case in the center.

To conform to the sealed standard sample adopted this date.

Adopted October 31, 1884.

S. B. HOLABIRD,
Quartermaster General, U. S. A.

2605—F., 1884.

DRUM CASE.

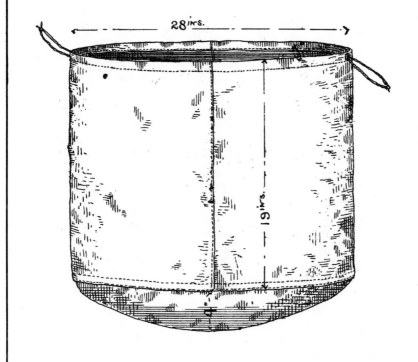

WAR DEPARTMENT,

QUARTERMASTER GENERAL'S OFFICE.

Specifications for Woolen Mittens.

To be of color of standard sample. To be made of gray woolen yarn, spun from long-staple wool of not less than one-half blood bred, free from shoddy, reworked wool, and other impurities, spun to weigh about seventy-three (73) grains for each twenty-five (25) yards of single thread ; the yarn to be doubled and twisted.

The mittens to be woven from sixteen (16) to eighteen (18) inches in length according to size, and fulled to the respective sizes, viz.: 10, 11, and 12 inches in length, and to be from $5\frac{1}{4}$ to 6 inches in width before being fulled.

To be manufactured in the following proportion of sizes to the one hundred—$\frac{40}{10}$, $\frac{36}{11}$, $\frac{24}{12}$ = 100.

The mittens when finished to weigh an average of three (3) pounds and six (6) ounces per dozen pairs.

Adopted November 6, 1884, in lieu of specifications of May 31, 1876, which are hereby canceled.

S. B. HOLABIRD,
Quartermaster General, U. S. A.

2617—F., 1884.

WOOLEN MITTENS.

0   3   6

WAR DEPARTMENT,

QUARTERMASTER GENERAL'S OFFICE.

Specifications for Company Marking Stamps.

The stamps to be of brass, one-half ($\frac{1}{2}$) inch high, eleven-sixteenths ($\frac{11}{16}$) of an inch wide, and of sufficient length for the inscription.

The face of stamps to bear the necessary inscription in letters and figures cut three thirty-seconds ($\frac{3}{32}$) of an inch deep; the prominent letters and figures to be one-half ($\frac{1}{2}$) inch long, and other letters one-quarter ($\frac{1}{4}$) inch long.

The stamp to be firmly connected by a rod to a walnut handle four and one-quarter ($4\frac{1}{4}$) inches long, mounted with a brass cap and ferrule.

The stamp to have a mortised end of sufficient size to contain two (2) numeral types, with a screw fitted in it to hold the types in place.

Two (2) sets of brass numerals, from o to 9 inclusive, of such dimensions and finish as to properly fit in the mortise of stamps and give an even impression with the stamp inscription, and to be furnished with each stamp, as also one marking pad, two and one-half ($2\frac{1}{2}$) inches wide and four and one-quarter ($4\frac{1}{4}$) inches long, and one (1) two (2) ounce bottle of warranted indelible ink.

The stamp, pad, bottle of ink, and sets of numerals to be put up in a substantial hinged-lid, japanned tin box four and one-quarter ($4\frac{1}{4}$) inches wide, eight (8) inches long, and one and one-quarter ($1\frac{1}{4}$) inches deep, arranged and finished according to sample in office of the Quartermaster General, U. S. A.

Adopted November, 29, 1884.

S. B. HOLABIRD,
Quartermaster General, U. S. A.

2845—F., 1884.

MARKING STAMP

Specifications for Woolen Blankets.

Wool.—To be pure long staple, free from shoddy, re-worked wool ·or cotton, or any impure materials. The warp to be of not lower grade than three-eighths ($\frac{3}{8}$) blood-bred wool; the filling or woof to be of not lower grade than one-half ($\frac{1}{2}$) blood-bred wool.

Size.—To be seven (7) feet long and five (5) feet six (6) inches wide.

Color.—To be blue and white mixed, conforming strictly to standard sample, with a dark-blue stripe two and one-half ($2\frac{1}{2}$) to three (3) inches wide across each end about six (6) inches from edge, the color of stripes to conform to those of the standard sample. The blue color in both warp and filling to be of *pure indigo dye* of best quality of ·indigo.

Weight.—To weigh not less than five (5) pounds.

Threads.—To have not less than twenty-two (22) threads of warp and twenty-five (25) threads of filling or woof to the inch. The threads to be well driven up.

Strength.—To bear a strain of not less than twenty-five (25) pounds per inch for the warp and thirty (30) pounds per inch for the woof without tearing.

U. S. Brand.—Each blanket to have the letters "U. S." four (4) inches long in the center, placed lengthwise with the blanket. The letters to be of pure indigo dye, and to conform in color to stripes, and may be either woven into the fabric or stamped on the blanket.

Finish.—To conform in all respects to the standard sample adopted this day.

Adopted January 9, 1885, *in lieu of specifications of February* 5, 1884, *which are hereby canceled.*

S. B. HOLABIRD,
Quartermaster General, U. S. A.

42—F., 1885.

WOOLEN BLANKET.

Specifications for Cavalry Guidons.

Silk.—To be of best quality of banner silk.

Size.—To be three (3) feet five (5) inches fly from the lance and two (2) feet three (3) inches on the lance; to be cut swallow-tailed fifteen (15) inches to the fork.

Design.—Two (2) horizontal stripes, each one-half (½) the width of flag, the upper to be red and the lower white. The upper stripe to have on both sides, in the center, the number of regiment in white silk, and the lower the letter of troop in red silk. The letter and number to be block-shaped, four and three-fourths (4¾) inches high, and held in place by a border of needle-work embroidery three-sixteenths ($\frac{3}{16}$) of an inch wide, of same color.

Lance.—To be one and one-fourth (1¼) inches in diameter and nine (9) feet long, including spear and ferrule.

Case or cover.—To be of water-proof material, to protect the guidon when furled.

Workmanship.—To conform to standard sample on file in the Quartermaster General's Office.

Adopted January 27, 1885.

S. B. HOLABIRD,
Quartermaster General, U. S. A.

245—F., 1885.

CAVALRY GUIDON.

WAR DEPARTMENT,

QUARTERMASTER GENERAL'S OFFICE.

Specifications for Barrack Bags.

Material.—To be made of six (6) ounce cotton duck, twenty-eight and one-half (28½) inches wide, dyed brown; to have drawing strings sixty (60) inches long, made of one-quarter (¼) inch braided cotton cord passing through two (2) sheet-brass grommets, one (1) on each side. To be sewed with No. 24 black cotton.

Size.—Thirty-two (32) inches deep and fifteen (15) inches in diameter.

Workmanship.—To be made flat stitched in the bottom and side seams; to have a tabling at the top two (2) inches wide for drawing strings, and conform to the sealed standard sample adopted this date.

Adopted March 9, 1885, in lieu of those of March 13, 1884, which are hereby canceled.

S. B. HOLABIRD,
Quartermaster General, U. S. A.

813—F., 1885.

BARRACK BAG.

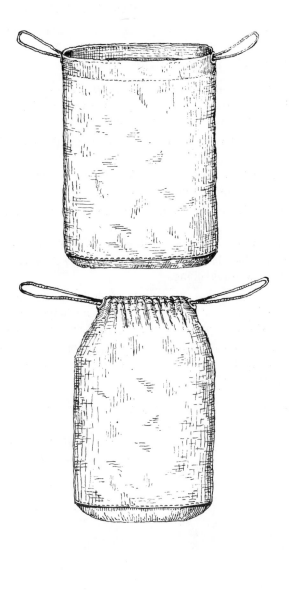

Specifications for Dark-blue Cloth-finished Blouse Flannel.

Wool.—To be pure long-staple American fleece wool of one-half (½) and three-quarters (¾) full blood, mixed in equal proportions, and free from shoddy, flocks, or other impurities.

Width.—To be fifty-four (54) inches, or six-fourths (6-4) of a yard wide.

Threads.—To contain not less than sixty (60) threads of warp and fifty-two (52) threads of filling in each square inch.

Weight.—To weigh not less than thirteen (13) ounces to the linear yard.

Strength.—To be capable of sustaining a strain of twenty-eight (28) pounds to the inch in width of warp, and twenty-three (23) pounds to the inch in width of filling.

Color.—To be of the same shade of dark blue as the standard sample, and to be dyed in the wool with pure indigo, best quality, unless otherwise authorized in writing by the contracting officer.

Finish.—To be twilled (kersey twill) nap well raised, cropped, steamed, closely shorn, well pressed, and finished in every way equal to the standard sample.

Adopted March 21, 1885, *in lieu of specifications of September* **29,** 1877, *which are hereby canceled.*

S. B. HOLABIRD,
Quartermaster General, U. S. A.

1002—F., 1885.

Specifications for Uniform Coat Buttons.

Size.—To be of two (2) sizes, designated as large and small. The large size to be thirty-two and one-half (32½) lignes, and the small size twenty-five (25) lignes.

Shell.—The shell of the large-size buttons to be made from gilding metal, number twenty-six (26) gauge. The small size to be of same metal number twenty-eight (28) gauge.

Backs.—The backs of both large and small size to be of soldering brass, number twenty-six (26) gauge.

Eye.—The eye of the large-size buttons to be of copper, number thirteen (13) gauge, and the small size of same metal, number fifteen (15) gauge.

Gilding.—The gilding to be done by fire process, and shell to be so treated that all gold shall be on outside surface. The weight of gold on each shell of the large-size buttons to be not less than four-fifths ($\frac{4}{5}$) of a pennyweight for each gross, and for the small size two-fifths ($\frac{2}{5}$) of a pennyweight for each gross.

Burnishing.—The burnishing to be done in the best manner known to the trade.

Stamping.—To be done with sharp, bright dies, free from any imperfections.

Solder.—The eye to be soldered into the back of the button with best quality spelter solder, and no backs to be used that show an abrasion around the eye.

Color.—To conform to standard sample.

Acid test.—To stand an acid test equal to standard samples.

Packing.—The buttons to be put up in gross boxes on cards of two two (2) dozen each. Each card to be protected by two (2) thicknesses of tissue paper.

Adopted March 27, 1885.

S. B. HOLABIRD,
Quartermaster General, U. S. A.

1065—F., 1885.

BUTTONS,

UNIFORM COAT.

EXCEPT FOR NON-COMMISSIONED STAFF OFFICERS.

SMALL.

LARGE.

WAR DEPARTMENT,

QUARTERMASTER GENERAL'S OFFICE.

Specifications for Mattresses.

To be equal in all respects to the sealed standard sample.

Material.—To be made of narrow stripe blue and white ticking; "herring-bone" or "twill" weave; the filling to be of good cotton linters.

Dimensions.—To be six (6) feet six (6) inches long, and two (2) feet eight (8) inches wide, and three and one-half (3½) inches deep when made up, and to weigh not less than twenty (20) pounds.

Workmanship.—To be made in a neat and substantial manner; to have twenty-eight (28) tufts of suitable quality of leather on the top and bottom.

Adopted March 28, 1885.

S. B. HOLABIRD,
Quartermaster General, U. S. A.

1075—F., 1885.

MATTRESS.

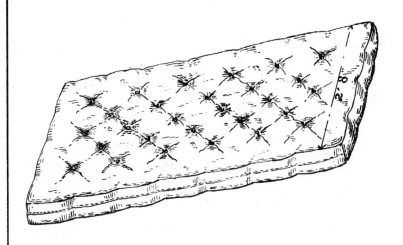

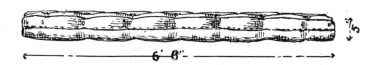

WAR DEPARTMENT,

QUARTERMASTER GENERAL'S OFFICE.

Specifications for Pillows.

To conform in all respects to the sealed standard sample.

Materials.—To be made of narrow striped blue and white ticking, "herring-bone" or "twill" weave; the filling to be of good cotton linters.

Dimensions.—To be thirty (30) inches long and seventeen (17) inches wide, and to weigh not less than three (3) pounds.

Workmanship.—To be made in a neat and substantial manner.

Adopted March 28, 1885.

S. B. HOLABIRD,
Quartermaster General, U. S. A.

1075—F., 1885.

88

PILLOW

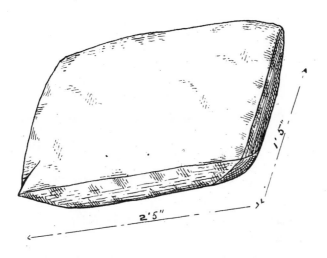

2'5"

1'5"

5½"

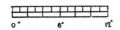

0"   6"   12"

WAR DEPARTMENT,

QUARTERMASTER GENERAL'S OFFICE

Specifications for Bed-sheets.

To conform in all respects to the sealed standard sample.

Material.—To be made of fine quality unbleached muslin.

Dimensions.—To be ninety (90) inches long and forty-eight (48) inches wide, when finished.

Workmanship.—To be made with a two (2) inch seam at the top and one (1) inch seam at the bottom, in a neat and substantial manner.

Adopted March 28, 1885.

S. B. HOLABIRD,
Quartermaster General, U. S. A.

1075—F., 1885.

SHEET.

4 FT

WAR DEPARTMENT,

QUARTERMASTER GENERAL'S OFFICE.

Specification for Muskrat Gauntlets.

To be made of muskrat skin, according to standard sample. Lining of lamb's fleece in hand, and blue or red cloth in gauntlet. Gauntlets to be at least five (5) inches deep, and of sufficient fullness to admit cuff of dress-coat or blouse. Palms of sheepskin conforming in quality to the standard sample.

To be of three (3) sizes, viz.: 9, 10, and 11.

Adopted April 3, 1885, in lieu of those of March 12, 1879, which are hereby canceled.

S. B. HOLABIRD,
Quartermaster General, U. S. A.

1137—F., 1885.

GAUNTLETS
MUSKRAT.

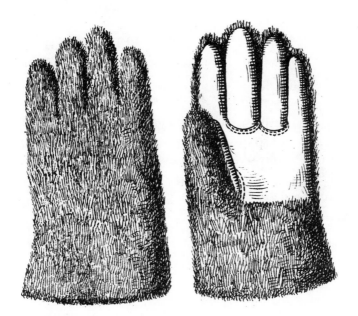

WAR DEPARTMENT,
QUARTERMASTER GENERAL'S OFFICE.

Specifications for Fly and Suspender Buttons.

To be equal in all respects to the sealed standard samples.

Size.—The fly buttons to be twenty-two (22) lignes; the suspender buttons to be twenty-seven (27) lignes.

Style.—To be what is called in the trade four (4) hole metal back, japanned fly and suspender buttons.

Packing.—To be put up in five (5) gross boxes.

Adopted April 14, 1885.

S. B. HOLABIRD,
Quartermaster General, U. S. A.

1332—F., 1885.

BUTTONS,
FLY AND SUSPENDER.

WAR DEPARTMENT,

QUARTERMASTER GENERAL'S OFFICE.

Specifications for "Markers" and "General Guides" for foot regiments.

MARKER.

Silk.—To be of best quality banner silk.

Size.—To be twenty (20) inches fly from the pike, and eighteen (18) inches on the pike.

Design.—Same as National Color, except that the stars are to be in two (2) circles, with one (1) star in each corner of the field. In the inner circle of stars, the number of regiment in solid block figures. Stars and figures to be white silk needlework embroidery on a single thickness of silk.

Pike.—To be of ash, and finished with brass spear-head and ferrule. Total length eight (8) feet.

Case or Cover.—To be of water-proof material, to protect the color when furled.

Workmanship.—To conform to standard sample in the office of the Quartermaster General, U. S. A.

GENERAL GUIDE.

Silk.—Same as for marker.

Size.—To be eighteen (18) inches fly from the rod casing, and fifteen (15) inches on the rod.

Design.—Same as for marker.

Trimming.—To be trimmed with yellow silk cut fringe, one and one-half (1½) inches deep.

Metal Rod and Spear-head.—Rod to be of brass tubing, nickel-plated, and of diameter to exactly fit inside the bore of a $\frac{45}{100}$ inch caliber rifle. To be twenty-eight and one-half (28½) inches long, with a collar fitted ten (10) inches from the bottom, to rest on the muzzle of the gun. To be finished at the proper places with two (2) nickel-plated knobs for fastening the flag, and at the top with a nickel-plated spear-head three and one-half (3½) inches long, conforming to standard sample.

Case or Cover.—Same as for marker.

Workmanship.—To conform to standard sample in the office of the Quartermaster General, U. S. A.

Adopted April 25, 1885.

S. B. HOLABIRD,

Quartermaster General, U. S. A.

1425—F., 1885.

MARKER AND GENERAL GUIDE.
FOOT REGIMENTS.

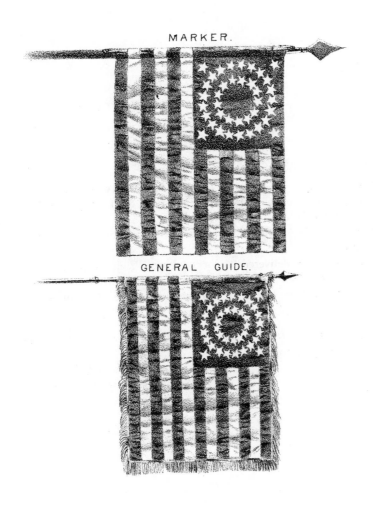

WAR DEPARTMENT,

QUARTERMASTER GENERAL'S OFFICE.

Specifications for Barrack Chairs.

The legs, slats, and rungs to be of clear hickory, well seasoned, ¼" or $\frac{5}{16}$" iron on each side, front and back; countersunk head on one end and a nut on the other.

The seat to be of raw-hide, secured with raw-hide throng lacing beneath.

The chairs to be delivered "knocked down," *i. e.*, not put together, but packed in crates of convenient size for transportation by rail.

To be packed in boxes for shipment over the "Union Pacific Railway."

Adopted May 5, 1885, *in lieu of specifications adopted October* 22, 1883, *which are hereby canceled.*

S. B. HOLABIRD,
Quartermaster General, U. S. A.

1296—F., 1885.

BARRACK CHAIR.

35½"

18½"

18½"

17½"

Specifications for Brassards.

Material.—To be made of white facing cloth, of Army standard quality.

Dimensions.—To be sixteen (16) inches long and three (3) inches wide when finished.

Design.—To be a strip of white cloth with sides turned under and stitched down with white silk. To have in the center a Greek cross two (2) inches by two (2) inches, made of scarlet facing cloth, edges of same to be stitched all around with scarlet silk.

Workmanship.—To conform to standard sample adopted this day.

Adopted June 30, 1885.

S., B. HOLABIRD,
Quartermaster General, U. S. A.

2248—F., 1885.

100

BRASSARD.

WAR DEPARTMENT,
Quartermaster General's Office.

Specifications for ⅘ Sky-blue Kersey—fine quality.

To be fifty-four (54) inches wide and to be made of not less than three-quarters (¾) blood bred wool, free from shoddy, flocks, or other impurities; to contain not less than seventy-six (76) threads of warp and sixty-eight (68) threads of filling to each square inch; to be capable of sustaining a strain of not less than fifty-eight (58) pounds to one inch width of warp and fifty (50) pounds to one inch width of filling.

To be woven like and finished equal to the standard sample.

The color to be the same shade of sky-blue as the standard sample, and to be dyed in the wool with pure indigo (unless otherwise authorized in writing by the contracting officer), and to have a yellow or white woolen list.

The kersey to weigh twenty-two (22) ounces per linear yard.

Adopted July 25, 1885.

S. B. HOLABIRD,
Quartermaster General, U. S. A.

2537—F., 1885.

WAR DEPARTMENT,

QUARTERMASTER GENERAL'S OFFICE.

Specifications for Gold Lace.

To be of the best quality gold on silver, the wire to weigh not less than ninety (90) grains to the linear yard of lace and to contain not less than 89 to 90 per cent. of silver and $1\frac{8}{10}$ to 2 per cent. gold.

To be full one-half ($\frac{1}{2}$) inch wide, and in weight, weave, finish, and all other respects to conform to standard sample.

The United States Mint assay to be the standard.

Adopted August 25, 1885, in lieu of specifications of January 28, 1885.

S. B. HOLABIRD,
Quartermaster General, U. S. A.

2793—F., 1885.

GOLD LACE
FOR CHEVRONS

WAR DEPARTMENT,

QUARTERMASTER GENERAL'S OFFICE.

Specifications for Blanket-lining Cloth.

To be fifty-four (54) inches or $\frac{6}{4}$ wide, and made of pure long-staple American fleece wool, of full one-quarter blood, combed and spun into soft yarn.

To contain not less than forty-four (44) threads in the filling and thirty (30) threads in the warp to each square inch, and to weigh not less than forty (40) ounces to the linear yard.

The cloth to be capable of standing a strain of not less than forty-five (45) pounds to the inch in width of warp, and fifty-four (54) pounds to the inch in width of filling.

To be dyed a fast black color, and the nap raised equal to the standard sample.

Adopted September 2, 1885.

S. B. HOLABIRD,
Quartermaster General, U. S. A.

2926—F., 1885.

WAR DEPARTMENT,
QUARTERMASTER GENERAL'S OFFICE.

Specifications for Buckles.

The buckle for Kersey trousers, overalls, and drawers to be of brass, seven-eighths ($\frac{7}{8}$) by one and one-quarter ($1\frac{1}{4}$) inches outside measure; the revolving bar carrying two (2) stout prongs, well let into the sides at a point five-sixteenths ($\frac{5}{16}$) of an inch from the outer bottom bar.

The buckle for White Linen trousers to be made of white metal, and to conform in size to the brass buckle above described.

Both to be equal in all respects to the sealed standard samples adopted this date.

Adopted September 12, 1885.

S. B. HOLABIRD,
Quartermaster General, U. S. A.

3077—F., 1885.

BUCKLES.

WHITE METAL.

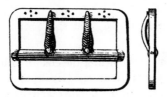

BRASS.

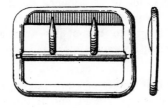

FULL SIZE.

WAR DEPARTMENT,

QUARTERMASTER GENERAL'S OFFICE.

Specifications for Regimental Colors—Infantry.

Material.—To be made of a single thickness of seamless blue banner silk of best quality.

Dimensions.—To be six (6) feet six (6) inches fly, by six (6) feet deep on the pike.

Design.—To bear in the center the coat of arms of the United States (as described in specifications for Cavalry standards). Underneath the eagle a red scroll with the number and name of regiment (as, for example, " 1st Regiment U. S. Infantry ") in white.

The coat of arms, scroll, numbers, and letters to be embroidered (needle work) in silk, the same on both sides of the Color, and in size, pattern, shades of color, and all other particulars to conform to standard sample in office of the Quartermaster General of the Army.

Trimming.—The Color to be trimmed on three sides with yellow silk knotted fringe two and one-half (2½) inches deep. One cord and tassels (total length to be not less than eleven and one-half (11½) feet), to accompany each Color, to be of blue and white silk intermixed.

Pike.—To be of best quality of ash, straight-grained and free from knots. To have a brass spear-head, and at the foot a brass ferrule to fit easily into the socket of the color sling. Total length nine (9) feet and ten (10) inches.

Cover.—To have an oil-cloth cover to fit easily over the Color when rolled on the pike.

Workmanship.—To conform to standard sample in office of the Quartermaster General of the Army.

Adopted September 14, 1885.

S. B. HOLABIRD,

Quartermaster General, U. S. A.

3066—F., 1885.

REGIMENTAL COLOR.

INFANTRY

WAR DEPARTMENT,

QUARTERMASTER GENERAL'S OFFICE.

Specifications for National Colors—Infantry and Artillery.

Material.—To be of best quality of banner silk.

Dimensions.—To be six (6) feet six (6) inches fly, by six (6) feet deep on the pike.

Design.—Thirteen (13) horizontal stripes of equal breadth, alternately red and white, beginning with the red. In the upper quarter next to the pike, a blue field of seamless banner silk thirty-one (31) inches long from the pike casing and extending down to the lower edge of the fourth red stripe from the top, with stars (one for each State) arranged horizontally in five (5) rows. The stars to be embroidered (needle work) in white silk, on both sides, and to be two and one-half (2½) inches from point to point.

Trimming.—The Colors to be trimmed on three sides with yellow silk knotted fringe two and one-half (2½) inches deep. One silk cord and tassels (total length to be not less than eleven and one-half (11½) feet) to accompany each Color; to be of blue and white silk intermixed for Infantry and red and yellow for Artillery.

Lettering.—The number and name of regiment (as, for example, "1st Regiment U. S. Infantry," "2d Regiment U. S. Artillery") to be embroidered in silk (needle work) on the center stripe in letters and figures two and one-half (2½) inches high. White for infantry, and yellow for Artillery.

Pike.—To be of best quality of ash, straight-grained and free from knots. To have a brass spear-head, and at the foot a brass ferrule to fit easily into the socket of the color sling. Total length nine (9) feet and ten (10) inches.

Cover.—To have an oil-cloth cover to fit easily over the Color when rolled on pike.

Workmanship.—To conform to standard sample in office of the Quartermaster General of the Army.

Adopted September 14, 1885.

S. B. HOLABIRD,
Quartermaster General, U. S. A.

3066—F., 1885.

WAR DEPARTMENT,
QUARTERMASTER GENERAL'S OFFICE.

Specifications for Sky-blue Kersey, heavy quality.

Wool.—To be of pure American fleece wool of not less than one-half blood bred, and free from shoddy, flocks, or other impurities.

Width.—To be fifty-four (54) inches, or $\frac{6}{4}$ wide.

Threads.—To contain not less than fifty (50) threads of warp and fifty-five (55) threads of filling in each square inch.

Weight.—To weigh not less than twenty-two (22) ounces to the linear yard.

Strength.—To be capable of sustaining a strain of sixty-five (65) pounds to the inch in width of warp and sixty (60) pounds to the inch in width of filling.

Color.—To be of same shade of blue as the standard sample, and to be dyed in the wool with pure indigo of best quality, unless otherwise authorized in writing by the contracting officer.

Finish.—The nap to be slightly raised; the finish to be equal in every way to the standard sample.

Adopted December 26, 1885, in lieu of specifications of July 2, 1875, which are hereby canceled.

S. B. HOLABIRD,
Quartermaster General, U. S. A.

3952—F., 1885.

WAR DEPARTMENT,

Specifications for White Metal Buttons for White Linen Trousers, Drawers, Overalls, Stable Frocks, etc.

To be equal in all respects to the sealed standard samples.

Size.—The small or fly buttons to be twenty-two (22) lignes, the large or suspender buttons to be twenty-seven (27) lignes.

Style.—To be what is called in the trade four (4) hole metal back, white metal fly and suspender buttons.

Packing.—To be put up in five (5) gross boxes.

Adopted January 12, 1886.

S. B. HOLABIRD,
Quartermaster General, U. S A.

43—F., 1886.

WAR DEPARTMENT,

QUARTERMASTER GENERAL'S OFFICE.

Specifications for Mattress-covers.

Duck.—To be made of cotton duck, forty (40) inches wide, weighing from eight and three-quarters (8¾) to nine (9) ounces to the linear yard.

To have fifty-three (53) threads of two-ply yarn to the inch of warp and thirty-four (34) threads of single yarn to the inch of filling.

To stand a breaking strain of not less than seventy (70) pounds to the half-inch of warp and not less than twenty-one (21) pounds to the half-inch of filling.

To be entirely free from sizing.

Dimensions.—Length when finished seventy-eight (78) inches. Width when finished thirty-nine (39) inches. The covers to have box corners four (4) inches deep.

Making.—The side seams to be felled down. The open end to have a two (2) inch hem, when finished. The top and bottom to overlap each other about one and a half (1½) inches at open end and be fastened by six (6) tapes, three-quarters (¾) of an inch wide and twelve (12) inches long, placed opposite each other on top and bottom sides, about nine (9) inches apart.

The covers, after being made up, to be smoothly pressed.

Materials, workmanship, and finish.—To be like and equal in all respects to the sealed standard sample.

Adopted January 20, 1886.

S. B. HOLABIRD,
Quartermaster General, U. S. A.

128—F.. 1886.

MATTRESS COVER.

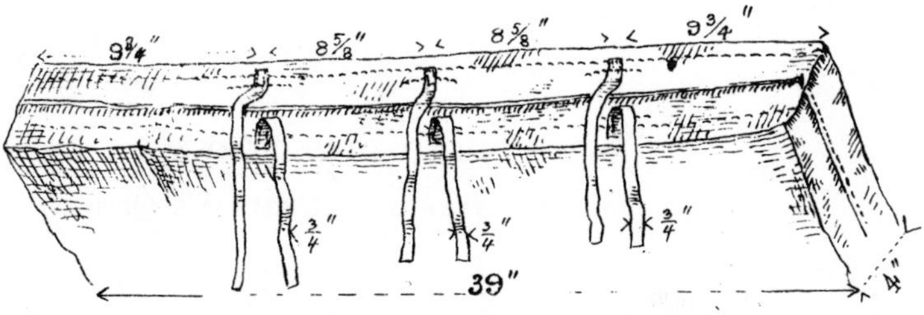

9¾″   8⅝″   8⅝″   9¾″

¾″   ¾″   ¾″

39″   4″

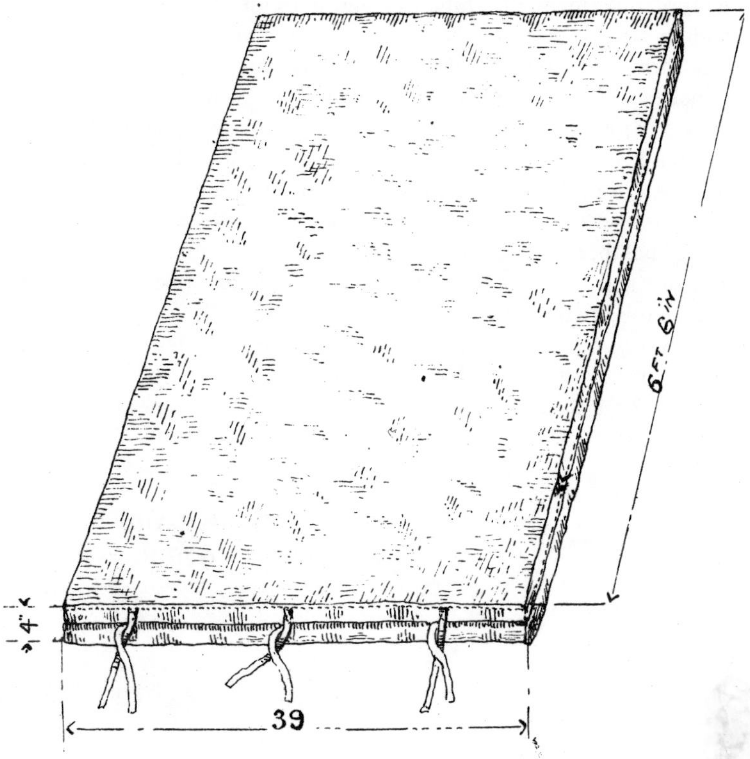

6 FT 6 IN

4″

39

Specifications for Improved Common Tent-poles.

Ridges to be made of white pine and uprights of ash.

Ridges six (6) feet ten (10) inches long, two and one-half (2½) inches wide, and one and seven-eights (1⅞) inches thick ; bands two (2) inches wide, of number twenty-four (24) galvanized iron, made with two (2) rivets, and secured to the pole by two (2) one (1) inch screws; a hole to admit a spindle one-half (½) inch in diameter, one and one-eighth (1⅛) inches to center from each end.

Uprights seven (7) feet four (4) inches long, two (2) inches thick ; bands of number twenty-four (24) galvanized iron, made with two (2) rivets, one and three-quarters (1¾) inches wide on upper end, secured to the pole by two (2) one (1) inch screws. Spindles of one-half (½) inch galvanized iron, to project three and one-quarter (3¼) inches and driven into the pole three (3) inches.

To conform to the standard sample. Three (3) poles (one ridge and two uprights) constitute a set.

Adopted January 30, 1886.

S. B. HOLABIRD,
Quartermaster General, U. S. A.

140—F., 1886.

Specifications for Campaign Shoes (with partly Machine Sewed Bottoms).

Material.—Uppers to be of the best quality of leather, oak-tanned, from slaughter hides.

Vamp, back, and *tongue* to be of wax-upper.

Inner counter to be of smooth wax-upper.

Middle counter to be of slaughter leather.

Soles to be of the best quality oak-tanned, from straight Texas hides, or from South American (commonly called "Spanish") dry hides.

Thread to be the best quality linen thread.

Nails used in heels to be $\frac{10}{8}$ Swede No. 12, 10 lbs. to the 100 pairs shoes, and ⅝ American iron, 5 lbs. to the 100 pairs shoes.

Sizes.—Nos. 5 to 12, inclusive.

The *width of the soles* across the ball of the foot to be as follows, and to be in proprotion throughout :—

SIZES.	5	6	7	8	9	10	11	12
	"	"	"	"	"	"	"	"
Letter "A"	3 5/16	3 7/16	3 9/16	3 11/16	3 13/16	3 15/16	4 1/16	4 3/16
Letter "B"	3⅜	3½	3⅝	3¾	3⅞	4	4⅛	4¼
Letter "C"	3 7/16	3 9/16	3 11/16	3 13/16	3 15/16	4 1/16	4 3/16	4 5/16

The *instep and ball* to measure as follows :—

SIZES.	5		6		7		8		9		10		11		12	
	Instep.	Ball.	Instep.	Ball.	Instep.	Ball.	Instep.	Ball.	Instep.	Ball.	Instep.	Ball.	Instep.	Ball.	Instep.	Ball.
	"	"	"	"	"	"	"	"	"	"	"	"	"	"	"	"
Letter "A"	8¾	8½	9	8¾	9¼	9	9½	9¼	9¾	9½	10	9¾	10¼	10	10½	10¼
Letter "B"	9	8¾	9¼	9	9½	9¼	9¾	9½	10	9¾	10¼	10	10½	10¼	10¾	10½
Letter "C"	9¼	9	9½	9¼	9¾	9½	10	9¾	10¼	10	10½	10¼	10¾	10½	11	10¾

Measurement for a No. 8 shoe, standard Letter "A," to be as follows: *Heel* 13⅛ inches, instep 9½ inches, ball and toe 9¼ inches, *height* of *back* at rear 5½ inches, *length of heel* 3 inches, *width of heel* 2⅞ inches, *height of heel* 1¼ inches, *width of sole or ball* 3¹¹⁄₁₆ inches.

Measurement for a No. 8 shoe, standard Letter "B," to be as Letter "A," with the following exceptions:—

Heel 13⅜ inches, *instep* 9¾ inches, *ball or toe* 9½ inches, *width of sole or ball* 3¾ inches.

Measurement for a No. 8 shoe, standard Letter "C," to be as Letter "A," with the following exceptions:—

Heel 13⅝ inches, *instep* 10 inches, *ball or toe* 9¾ inches, *width of sole or ball* 3¹³⁄₁₆ inches.

Workmanship.—*Vamp and back* to be crimpled; *tongue* to be hand-sewed to the vamp with a flat seam; *inner counter* to be neatly skived around the upper edge and to be fastened to the back with 3-cord waxed linen thread, nine (9) stitches to the inch. The *inner sole, upper,* and *welt* to be fastened together with twelve (12) cord wax sole thread, four (4) stitches to the inch. *Outer sole and welt* to be fastened together with ten (10) cord wax sole thread, seven (7) stitches to the inch. To be worked square with the last. The edges to be finished with pressers without heel-ball, and to measure at least half a size (outside) more than they are marked.

Adopted April 27, 1886 in lieu of specifications of July 14, 1885, which are hereby canceled.

S. B. HOLABIRD,
Quartermaster General, U. S. A.

540—F., 1886.

WAR DEPARTMENT,

QUARTERMASTER GENERAL'S OFFICE.

Specifications for Ax-helves.

To be thirty-six (36) inches long, and made of good, seasoned, straight-grained hickory, free from knots or shakes.

To be polished and have a saw-cut (to receive a wedge) two and a half (2½) to three (3) inches deep on the end fashioned to fit the eye of the Ax.

To be equal in all respects to the sealed standard sample.

Adopted March 17, 1886, in lieu of specifications of May 31, 1876, which are hereby canceled.

S. B. HOLABIRD,
Quartermaster General, U. S. A.

595—F., 1886.

AXE HELVES.

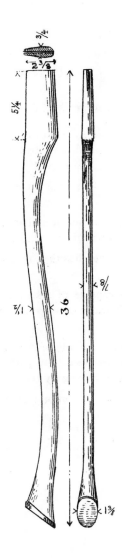

WAR DEPARTMENT,

QUARTERMASTER GENERAL'S OFFICE.

Specifications for Dark-blue Cloth—fine quality.

Wool.—To be of pure American fleece wool of not less than three-quarters (¾) to full blood, and free from shoddy, flocks, or other impurities.

Width.—To be fifty-four (54) inches or six-fourths (⁶⁄₄) of a yard wide.

Threads.—To contain not less than eighty (80) threads of warp and seventy-four (74) threads of filling to the square inch.

Weight.—To weigh not less than nineteen (19) ounces to the linear yard.

Strength.—To be capable of sustaining a strain of forty-two (42) pounds to the inch in width of warp and thirty (30) pounds to the inch in width of filling.

Color.—To be of same shade of dark-blue as the standard sample, and to be dyed in the wool with pure indigo, best quality, (unless otherwise authorized in writing by the contracting officer).

Weave and finish.—To conform in all respects to the standard sample.

Adopted April 13, 1886.

S. B. HOLABIRD,
Quartermaster General, U. S. A.

823—F., 1886.

126

WAR DEPARTMENT,

QUARTERMASTER GENERAL'S OFFICE.

Specifications for Regimental Colors, Artillery.

Material.—To be made of a single thickness of seamless scarlet silk, of quality and exact shade of color of that in the sealed standard sample.

Dimensions.—To be six (6) feet six (6) inches fly by six (6) feet deep on the pike.

Design.—To bear in the center two cannon crossing, with the letters " U. S." above in a scroll, and, underneath, the number of regiment (as, for example, " First Regiment Artillery "), also in a scroll. The scrolls to be of yellow and the letters of scarlet.

The crossed cannon, scrolls and letters to be embroidered (needle-work) in silk, the same on both sides of the color, and in size, pattern, shades of color and all other particulars to conform to standard sample in Office of the Quartermaster General of the Army.

Trimmings.—The color to be trimmed on three sides with yellow silk knotted-fringe two and one-half (2½) inches deep. One cord and tassels (total length to be not less than eleven and one-half (11½) feet) to accompany each color, to be of scarlet and yellow silk intermixed.

Pike.—To be of best quality of ash, straight grained, and free from knots. To have a brass spear-head, and at the foot a brass ferrule to fit easily into the socket of the color sling. Total length nine (9) feet and ten (10) inches.

Cover.—To have an oil-cloth cover to fit easily over the color when rolled on the pike.

Workmanship.—To conform to the sealed standard sample in the Office of the Quartermaster General of the Army.

Adopted April 29, 1886.

S. B. HOLABIRD,
Quartermaster General, U. S. A.

914—F., 1886.

129

WAR DEPARTMENT,

QUARTERMASTER GENERAL'S OFFICE.

Specifications for Leather Gauntlets.

To be of Angora goat-skin. The gauntlet or cuff to be at least four and one-half (4½) inches deep, and of sufficient fullness to admit cuff of coat.

The cuff to be lined with russet leather.

The gloves to be "table cut," and the seams well stitched throughout with linen thread. The seams in the thumb and between the fingers to be welted.

The cuff and back of glove to be stitched with silk, as in standard sample.

In quality of material and workmanship they must conform to the standard sample.

To be of five sizes, and put up in the following proportion to the 100 pairs: Ten, 8; twenty-three, 8½; thirty, 9; twenty-two, 9½; fifteen, 10.

Adopted May 11, 1886, in lieu of specifications of May 21, 1884, which are hereby canceled.

S. B. HOLABIRD,
Quartermaster General, U. S. A.

1018—F., 1886.

130

LEATHER GAUNTLETS.

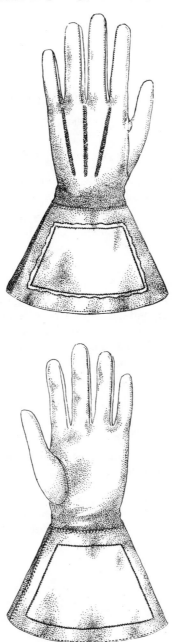

WAR DEPARTMENT,

QUARTERMASTER GENERAL'S OFFICE.

Specifications for Artillery Guidons.

Silk.—To be a single piece of best quality of banner silk of exact shade of scarlet as the standard sample.

Size.—To be three (3) feet five (5) inches fly from the lance, and two (2) feet three (3) inches on the lance; to be cut swallow-tailed fifteen (15) inches to the fork.

Design.—To bear in the center, on both sides of the guidon, two cannon crossing (about fourteen and one-half ($14\frac{1}{2}$) inches in length), with the number of regiment above and letter of battery below. The crossed cannon, letter, and number to be of yellow silk, and to be held in place by a border of needle-work embroidery three-sixteenths ($\frac{3}{16}$) of an inch wide, of same color. The letter and number to be block-shaped, four and one-half ($4\frac{1}{2}$) inches high.

Lance.—To be one and one-fourth ($1\frac{1}{4}$) inches in diameter and nine (9) feet long, including spear and ferrule.

Case or Cover.—To be of waterproof material to protect the guidon when furled.

Workmanship.—To conform to standard sample on file in the Quartermaster General's Office.

Adopted May 21, 1886.

S. B. HOLABIRD,
Quartermaster General, U. S. A.

109c—**F.**, 1886.

133

WAR DEPARTMENT,

QUARTERMASTER GENERAL'S OFFICE.

Specifications for Canvas Caps.

Material.—To be made of six (6) ounce cotton duck, dyed brown, lined with light blanket cloth next the duck, and with scarlet flannel in the inside; to have two buttons on the cape to button at the throat, and one, vest size, brown "lasting" button on the top for finish. The visor and edges bound with ¾ brown cotton tape.

Style.—Scull cap with extension forming a cape reaching to the shoulders and meeting in front, covering the throat, and buttoning together with two (2) buttons. A visor of the same material bound with ¾ brown cotton tape sewed on the forehead (to be worn up or down as desired), and having hook and eye to fasten it when turned up.

Workmanship.—To be cut and made in conformity with the sealed standard sample adopted this date.

Adopted June 22, 1886, in lieu of specifications of April 17, 1884, which are hereby canceled.

S. B. HOLABIRD,
Quartermaster General, U. S. A.

1281—F., 1886.

CANVAS CAP.

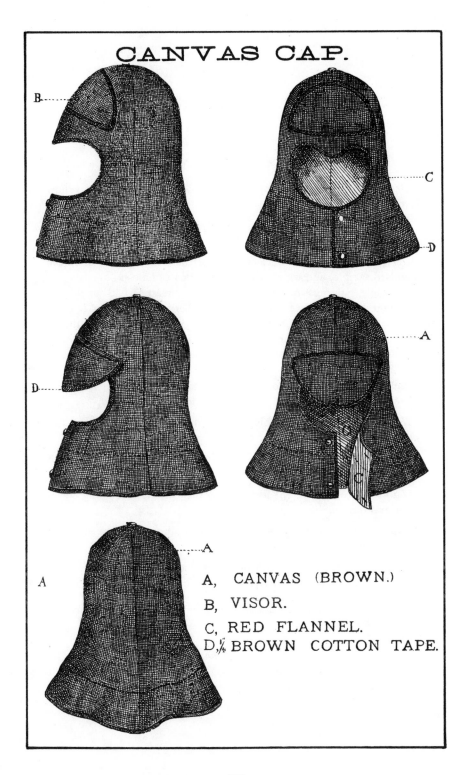

A, CANVAS (BROWN.)

B, VISOR.

C, RED FLANNEL.

D,¾ BROWN COTTON TAPE.

Specifications for Cavalry Standards.

Material.—To be made of a single thickness of seamless yellow banner-silk.

Dimensions.—To be four (4) feet fly, and three (3) feet on the lance.

Design.—To have the Coat of Arms of the United States as on the Standard sample, and which may be described as follows :

An eagle with outstretched wings; on its breast a U. S. shield; in the right talon an olive branch with red berries, and in his left ten (10) arrows bunched. A red scroll held in eagle's beak, with the motto, "E Pluribus Unum," in yellow; over the scroll a group of thirteen (13) white stars, surmounted by an arc of diverging sun-rays, also in white.

Below the eagle a red scroll with the number and name of Regiment in yellow, as for example " 3d U. S. Cavalry."

Embroidery.—The design, letters, and figures to be embroidered in silk, the same on both sides of the standard.

Trimming.—The standard to be trimmed on three (3) sides with U. S. silk-knotted fringe, two and one-half (2½) inches deep.

Lance.—To be nine (9) feet, six (6) inches long, including metal spear and ferrule.

Case or Cover.—To be of waterproof material to protect the Standard when furled.

Workmanship.—To conform in all respects to the standard sample on file in the Quartermaster General's Office.

Adopted July 7, 1886, in lieu of those of February 4, 1884, which are hereby canceled.

S. B. HOLABIRD,
Quartermaster General, U. S. A.

1390—P., 1886.

CAVALRY STANDARD.

WAR DEPARTMENT,

QUARTERMASTER GENERAL'S OFFICE.

Specifications for Drums, complete.

Pattern.—To be according to standard sample and to weigh, complete, about four (4) pounds and ten (10) ounces.

Wood shell.—Maple veneered, stained to imitate rose-wood and polished; sixteen (16) inches in diameter, and including hoops, eight and three-eighths (8⅜) inches high. Two (2) hoops, each one and three-eighths (1⅜) inches in width, stained and polished black.

There should be painted on the outside of the shell of each drum, the escutcheon of the Arms of the United States, and upon the field of the same, the letters " U. S." in gilt, seven-eighths (⅞) of an inch long, and the contractor's name, with date of contract, on the inside of the shell, visible from the vent.

Two (2) calf-skin heads, one (1) batter and one (1) snare. One (1) set of snares of eight (8) strands, snares attached to drum by a long adjustable nickel-plated snare-screw fastened to both hoops. Eight (8) steel tightening rods with double hooks rigidly affixed to the end thereof, with a six (6) squared coupling sleeve, threaded over the free end of the rod, and another double hook swivelled to the outer end of this coupling sleeve.

Belt hooks.—Of stout brass wire, fastened to lugs on two (2) parallel rod hooks.

Knee rest.—Composed of two (2) brass wire carrying frames, pivoted to fall towards and open away from each other in a plane nearly parallel with the drum heads, with a flexible crimson leather strap connecting the free ends of said frames, is attached to the lower end of two (2) adjacent tightening rods.

All metal parts of the drum to be nickel-plated.

Two (2) nickel-plated wrenches to accompany each drum.

Adopted July 9, 1886, in lieu of specifications of January 15, 1883, which are hereby canceled.

S. B. HOLABIRD,
Quartermaster General, U. S. A.

1047—F., 1886.

DRUM.

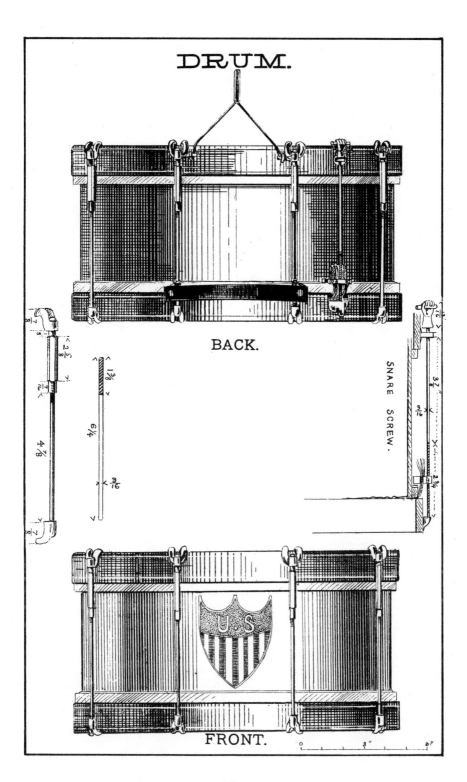

BACK.

SNARE SCREW.

FRONT.

139

DRUM.

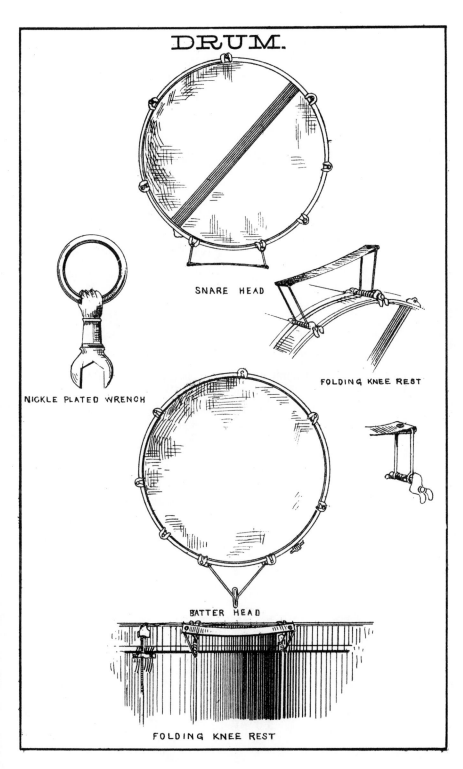

SNARE HEAD

NICKLE PLATED WRENCH

FOLDING KNEE REST

BATTER HEAD

FOLDING KNEE REST

WAR DEPARTMENT,
QUARTERMASTER GENERAL'S OFFICE.

Specifications for Pillow-cases.

To conform in all respects to the sealed standard sample.

Material.—To be made of fine quality unbleached muslin.

Dimensions.—To be thirty-six (36) inches long and eighteen and one-half (18½) inches wide, when finished.

Workmanship.—To be made in a neat and substantial manner, and to have a two (2) inch seam at the top.

Adopted October 16, 1886, *in lieu of specifications of March* 28, 1885, *which are hereby canceled.*

S. B. HOLABIRD,
Quartermaster General, U. S. A.

1286—F., 1886.

PILLOW CASE.

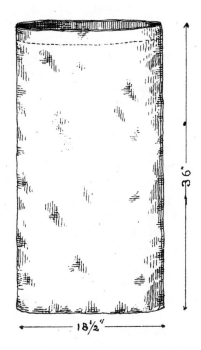

36"

18½"

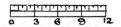

0   3   6   9   12

WAR DEPARTMENT,

Quartermaster General's Office.

Specifications for Suspenders.

Front Straps.—The front straps are to be made of non-elastic webbing ¾ inch broad, to have thirteen cords, and to be of weight and quality of the standard sample. They are to be attached directly to the buckle in the manner known as " Cantab," and before they are sewed together; to be 9½ inches long, and overlap each other to an extent that will give sufficient "play" or change of length of the two straps that are fastened together; the parts of the straps that overlap each other on the rollers of the buckle to be reinforced with sheepskin leather of weight and quality of standard sample. The button-hole is to be woven into the strap and must be at least half an inch from the extremity of the strap.

Shoulder-straps.—The shoulder-straps are to be made of one continuous piece of non-elastic webbing folded and bent upon itself in the middle, as per sample. They are to be 1⅜ inches broad, of same weight, and be equal in quality in every respect to the standard sample ; to be regular in width and weaving, and to have a figure woven on them equal to sample. The extremities to be neatly bound.

Back Straps.—The back straps are to be made of elastic rubber web, to have twenty-two cords and to be 1¼ inches broad. The rubber thread is to be that made by the East Hampton Rubber Co., or other equally as good, of the size known to the trade as No. 28, and to be freshly manufactured. The button-holes are to be woven into the strap and to be at least ⅞ of an inch from the extremity of the strap or end. The straps are to be neatly woven, with a smooth even face, and edges to be neatly bound at the ends, the binding to extend up one-half the length of button-hole on each side.

Buckle.—The buckle is to be made in one piece and be stamped from sheet brass of weight equal to that on sample, and to have three prongs. It must have an opening sufficient to accommodate the shoulder-straps, and two smaller openings or slots of a size that will allow the cantab straps to freely play or move through it. Each slot must have an anti-friction roller to prevent the wear of the strap upon the buckle, as on sample. Both the friction rollers and the prongs must be made from brass, well nickel plated.

Re-inforce Straps.—The back straps to be united to the shoulder-straps by two rows of stitching, as shown on sample. The shoulder-straps are also to be fastened together in the back by a re-inforce or strengthening piece made from web similar to the shoulder-straps, of the size and shape of sample, with its cut edges bound, the strengthening-piece securely sewed to the shoulder-straps, as in sample. The front straps will be sewed by four lines of stitching nearly forming a square, as per sample.

Button-hole strengthening.—All the button-holes are to be strengthened by being whipped or over-sewed at their wearing extremities, to the extent of the sample.

Lengths.—The suspenders are to be of three lengths, and to measure from the extremes of the front and back button-holes 36 inches, 38 inches, and 40 inches, respectively.

Thread.—All the thread used in sewing the suspenders must be made from the Sea-island cotton and be of the best quality.

Color.—All the parts of the suspender must be of the same color and must be " fast " color, and as per samples.

Packing.—The suspenders must be neatly packed in paper boxes, one dozen of the same size in a box.

Each pair of suspenders is to have the length of same stamped or stenciled in black or blue color on the reverse side of the strengthening-strap (without however defacing the outer side) in letters and figures ⅜ of an inch long, as follows :—

40-in.

38-in.

36-in.

Adopted February 25, 1887, *in lieu of those of September* 4, 1883, *which are hereby canceled.*

S. B. HOLABIRD,
Quartermaster General, U. S. A.

363—F., 1887.

SUSPENDER.

Specifications for Blouse-lining Flannel.

Materials.—The warp to be made of the best long-staple American cotton yarn, No. 40, doubled and twisted, dyed pure indigo blue, and to weigh one and three-quarters (1¾) ounces to the yard. The filling to weigh four and one-quarter (4¼) ounces to the yard, and be composed of good quality American fleece wool, at least one-quarter blood, and of the best long-staple American cotton, in the proportion of seventy-five (75) parts wool to twenty-five (25) parts cotton, and to be free from shoddy, flocks, or other impurities. The wool of the filling to be dyed with pure indigo, and the cotton with a fast dye.

Width.—To be full twenty-seven (27) inches wide when finished.

Threads.—To have fifty-six (56) threads of warp and forty-eight (48) threads of filling to the inch (square).

Strength.—The breaking strain to be not less than forty (40) pounds to one inch width of warp and thirty-eight (38) pounds to one inch of filling in the piece.

Weight.—The goods when finished to weigh not less than six (6) ounces to the linear yard.

Color.—To conform to standard sample.

Finish.—To be neither hot nor cold pressed, and to be properly fulled.

Adopted April 2, 1887, *in lieu of specifications of March* 19, 1883, *which are hereby canceled.*

S. B. HOLABIRD,
Quartermaster General, U. S. A.

671—F., 1887.

WAR DEPARTMENT,

QUARTERMASTER GENERAL'S OFFICE.

Specifications for Boots (with partly machine sewed bottoms).

Material.—Uppers to be of the best quality oak-tanned from slaughter hides, the leg to be finished on the grain.

Straps to be made of calf-skin or smooth-wax upper.

Vamp and outside *counter* to be of wax-upper.

Soles of best quality oak-tanned, from straight Texas hides, or from South American (commonly called "Spanish") dry hides; no split leather to be used.

Thread to be the best quality silk and linen thread.

Nails used in heels to be $\frac{11}{8}$ Swede No. 12, 10 lbs. to the 100 pairs boots, and $\frac{5}{8}$ American iron, 5 lbs. to the 100 pairs boots.

Sizes.—Nos. 5 to 12, inclusive.

The width of the soles across the ball of the foot to be as follows, and to be in proportion throughout:

SIZES.	5	6	7	8	9	10	11	12
Letter "A"	$3\frac{5}{16}$	$3\frac{7}{16}$	$3\frac{9}{16}$	$3\frac{11}{16}$	$3\frac{13}{16}$	$3\frac{15}{16}$	$4\frac{1}{16}$	$4\frac{3}{16}$
Letter "B"	$3\frac{3}{8}$	$3\frac{1}{2}$	$3\frac{5}{8}$	$3\frac{3}{4}$	$3\frac{7}{8}$	4	$4\frac{1}{8}$	$4\frac{1}{4}$
Letter "C"	$3\frac{7}{16}$	$3\frac{9}{16}$	$3\frac{11}{16}$	$3\frac{13}{16}$	$3\frac{15}{16}$	$4\frac{1}{16}$	$4\frac{3}{16}$	$4\frac{5}{16}$

The instep and ball to measure as follows:

SIZES.	5		6		7		8		9		10		11		12	
	Instep.	Ball.	Instep.	Ball.	Instep.	Ball.	Instep.	Ball.	Instep.	Ball.	Instep.	Ball.	Instep.	Ball.	Instep.	Ball.
Letter "A"	$8\frac{3}{4}$	$8\frac{1}{2}$	9	$8\frac{3}{4}$	$9\frac{1}{4}$	9	$9\frac{1}{2}$	$9\frac{1}{4}$	$9\frac{3}{4}$	$9\frac{1}{2}$	10	$9\frac{3}{4}$	$10\frac{1}{4}$	10	$10\frac{1}{2}$	$10\frac{1}{4}$
Letter "B"	9	$8\frac{3}{4}$	$9\frac{1}{4}$	9	$9\frac{1}{2}$	$9\frac{1}{4}$	$9\frac{3}{4}$	$9\frac{1}{2}$	10	$9\frac{3}{4}$	$10\frac{1}{4}$	10	$10\frac{1}{2}$	$10\frac{1}{4}$	$10\frac{3}{4}$	$10\frac{1}{2}$
Letter "C"	$9\frac{1}{4}$	9	$9\frac{1}{2}$	$9\frac{1}{4}$	$9\frac{3}{4}$	$9\frac{1}{2}$	10	$9\frac{3}{4}$	$10\frac{1}{4}$	10	$10\frac{1}{2}$	$10\frac{1}{4}$	$10\frac{3}{4}$	$10\frac{1}{2}$	11	$10\frac{3}{4}$

Measurement for a No. 8 boot, standard, *Letter " A,"* to be as follows : *Heel* 13⅛ inches, *instep* 9½ inches, *ball or toe* 9¼ inches, *length of leg* 19 inches in front, 14 inches back, *width of leg* at top 15 inches, *width of strap* 1¼ inches, *length of strap* 7 inches, *height of counter* 3 inches, *width of heel* 2⅞ inches, *length of heel* 3 inches, *height of heel* 1¼ inches, *width of sole or ball* 3$\frac{11}{16}$ inches.

Measurement for a No. 8 boot, standard, *Letter " B,"* to be as Letter " A," with the following exceptions :

Heel 13⅜ inches, *instep* 9¾ inches, *ball or toe* 9½ inches, *width of sole or ball* 3¾ inches.

Measurement for a No. 8 boot, standard, *Letter " C,"* to be as Letter " A," with the following exceptions :

Heel 13⅝ inches, *instep* 10 inches, *ball or toe* 9¾ inches, *width of sole or ball* 3$\frac{13}{16}$ inches.

Workmanship.—The leg to be cut in two pieces, with lap seam in front ; to be stitched with three (3) rows of stitching, ten (10) stitches to the inch ; the upper stitching to be of heavy silk thread, the under stitching to be of best quality linen thread. Back seam to be covered with a strip of same material as leg, to measure one (1) inch in width at top and two (2) inches in width at counter. Counter to be stitched to leg with five (5) cord waxed linen thread, six (6) stitches to the inch.

The strap to be sewed to the inside of the leg with five (5) cord waxed linen thread, six (6) stitches to the inch. The vamp and outside counter to be stitched on to the leg with three (3) rows of stitching, ten (10) stitches to the inch, the upper stitching to be of heavy silk thread, the under stitching to be of the best quality linen thread. The back seam to be sewed with five (5) cord waxed linen thread, six (6) stitches to the inch. The inner sole, welt, and upper to be fastened together with twelve (12) cord wax sole thread, four (4) stitches to the inch. The outer sole and welt to be fastened together with ten (10) cord wax sole thread, seven stitches to the inch. To be worked square with the last, the edges to be finished with pressers without heel-ball, and to measure at least half a size (outside) more than they are marked. The feather of the inner sole to be rounded.

Adopted March 14, 1887, *in lieu of specifications of April* 27, 1886, *which are hereby canceled.*

S. B. HOLABIRD,
Quartermaster General, U. S. A.

512—F., 1887.

WAR DEPARTMENT,

QUARTERMASTER GENERAL'S OFFICE.

Specifications for Linen Collars.

Style.—To be four-ply standing collars, conforming in height and shape to sealed standard sample.

Materials.—The outside surface to be of pure 2,000 Irish linen. The two inter-linings and facing to be of material like and equal to that of the sealed standard sample.

Workmanship and Finish.—The stitching to be 22 to the inch. The collars to be " Combination " turned, to be properly laundried, and to conform in all other respects to the sealed standard sample.

Sizes.—To run from 14 to 18, inclusive, in such proportions as required.

Adopted March 24, 1887.

S. B. HOLABIRD,
Quartermaster General, U. S. A.

585—F , 1887.

LINEN COLLAR.

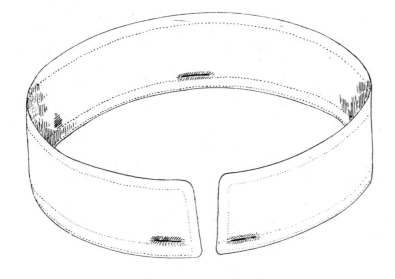

Specifications for Music Pouches—Large and Small.

Sizes.—To be made in two sizes, known as large and small. The pouch or box part of the larger size to be seven (7) inches long, nine (9) inches wide, one and one-half (1½) inches deep. The pouch or box part of the small size to be six and three-quarters (6¾) inches long, five and one-quarter (5¼) inches wide, and one and one-quarter (1¼) inches deep.

Material and Make.—The body to be made of black enameled leather, first quality, covered with dark-blue cloth weighing 16 ounces to the yard, firmly glued and stitched to the leather; the cloth to be turned over the edge of the leather in the box part ¾ of an inch and on the flap ⅜ of an inch; the flap to have two rows of stitching—one row close to the outer edge of the "turn in," the other row $\frac{3}{16}$ of an inch apart from the first row. The flap to be fashioned and finished with an edging of (real) gold lace $\frac{9}{32}$ of an inch wide (known in the trade as No. 1962), in accordance with the standard sample. The ends to be made of black patent leather ⅛ of an inch thick, firmly and neatly stitched to the body of the pouch, eight stitches to the inch, this stitching forming a finish to the box part of the pouch. In the center of the rounded bottom of the pouch a brass "nib," with a shoulder, is to be riveted over a copper burr on the inside, the nib to be $\frac{3}{16}$-inch stem, having an oval head $\frac{5}{16}$-inch, the flap to be furnished with a leather strap 3½ x 1¼ inches, securely stitched to the under side of the same with a hole punched therein to receive the nib. On the back near the top, and at proper angles, are to be placed two triangles, brass, ⅞-inch, held in place by black enameled leather straps securely and neatly stitched to the pouch.

Carrying Strap or Sling.—The carrying strap to be made of first quality black enameled leather, one (1) inch wide, rounded edges, and made in two parts; the long part 41½ inches long, the short part 13 inches long, including the "turn-in" for snaps and buckle; each part to be furnished with a gilt spring-snap on one end, and put on with gilt screw-studs with ½-inch heads; the other end of the long part to have five eyelet-holes for tongue of buckle, the first hole 3½ inches from the end and the others 1 inch from centers; one end of the short or adjusting part of the strap to be furnished with a gilt buckle 1 inch square. The face of the carrying strap to be finished with a band of (real) gold lace $1\frac{3}{16}$ inch wide (known in the trade as No. 2043), neatly stitched on with yellow silk. The center of this band of gold lace to have a row of stitching $\frac{1}{8}$ inch wide, of the various colors denoting the arms of the service, in the proportion for each arm, as may be required.

To conform in all respects to the standard samples.

Adopted April 5, 1887.

S. B. HOLABIRD,
Quartermaster General, U. S A.

704—F., 1887.

MUSIC POUCH.

LARGE.

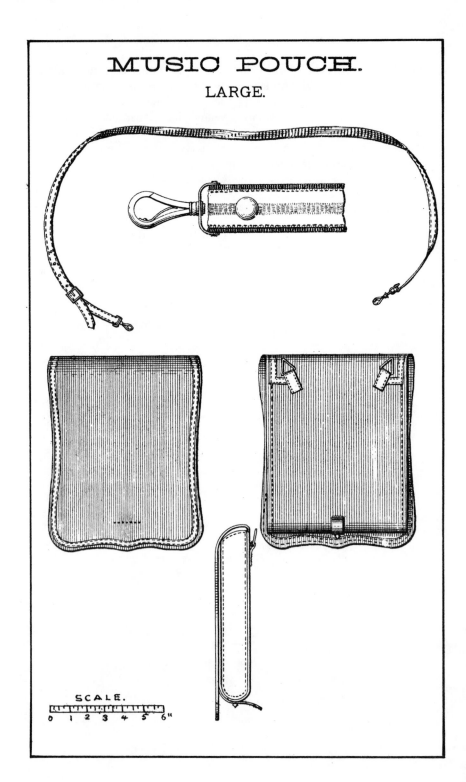

SCALE.

0 1 2 3 4 5 6"

MUSIC POUCH.

SMALL.

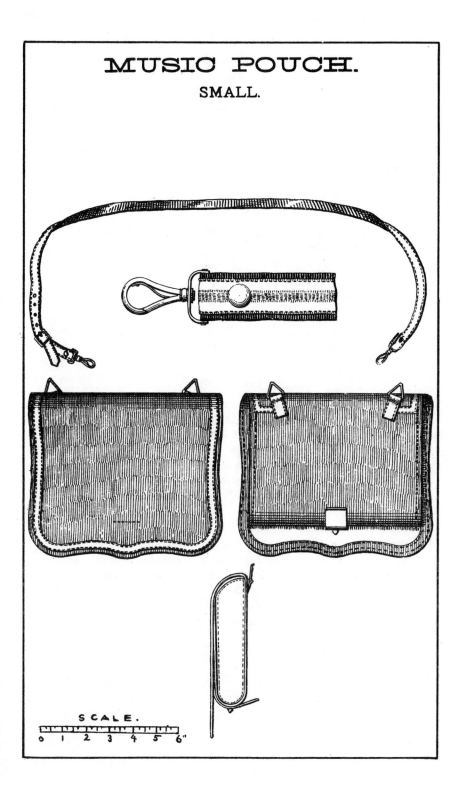

SCALE.

0 1 2 3 4 5 6"

Specifications for Shoulder-knot and Aiguillette.

KNOTS.

Cord.—To be U. S. gauge 5, made on 16 carrier machine, of two-end No. 26, two-fold worsted, ⅜ blood stock, filling of cotton.

Tin.—Tin form, 6¼ x 2¾ inches, extremes. Brass hook, 1¾ inches, No. 14 wire, double.

Upper.—Twilled cloth.

Lining.—Twilled muslin or chintz.

Lacet.—Cotton.

Button.—Small coat, Army standard. The Knot to be fashioned over the cushioned tin form in three-cord net work, in accordance with the standard sample.

AIGUILLETTE.

Cord.—To be U. S. gauge 3, made on 24 carrier machine, of two-end No. 26, two-fold worsted, ⅜ blood stock, filling of cotton. To be passed over the plate and under the net work of the right shoulder-knot; a loop to be formed on each side, the back loop to be 15 inches long, and the front loop 17 inches long, clear of the knot. The back part of the aiguillette to be loop-plaited for 30 inches of its length from the knot, then extending in single cord 5 inches from plait, at which point a coil of five laps is made and the end passed through this coil and extended in single cord 4½ inches, and finished with a brass-gilt tip 3¼ inches long; at top of coil is a small worsted cord-loop for button. The front part of aiguillette is to be made in the same manner as the back part except that the portion to be loop-plaited is 22 inches, from which the single cord extension is six inches to the coil. The knots and aiguillettes to be dyed fast colors, and to conform in all respects to the sealed standard sample.

Adopted April 5, 1887.

S. B. HOLABIRD,
Quartermaster General, U. S. A.

704—F., 1887.

156

AIGUILLETTE
WITH SHOULDER KNOTS.

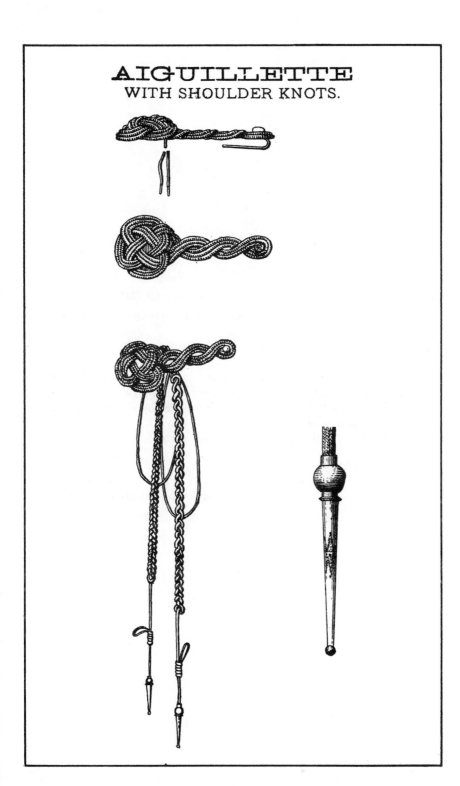

WAR DEPARTMENT,

QUARTERMASTER GENERAL'S OFFICE.

Specifications for Lyres.

To be made of German silver, fifteen per cent. fine, with two brass-wire prongs ¾ inch long securely soldered on the back of the device.

To be one and three-sixteenths ($1\frac{3}{16}$) inches by eleven-sixteenths ($\frac{11}{16}$) of an inch at extremes.

To conform in all respects to the standard sample.

Adopted April 5, 1887.

S. B. HOLABIRD,
Quartermaster General, U. S. A.

704—F., 1887.

WAR DEPARTMENT,

QUARTERMASTER GENERAL'S OFFICE.

Specifications for Hair Plumes for Helmets.

To be made of good horse-hair dyed a fast color to shade of standard sample.

To droop from top of socket over back and sides of helmet.

The hairs are woven and sewed together at one end, giving the latter the form of a flattened knob about one and five-eighths (1⅝) inches diameter, with star-shaped brass eyelet in center to admit the pen of the top piece. Length of plume from eyelet to end fourteen (14) inches.

Adopted April 5, 1887.

S. B. HOLABIRD,
Quartermaster General, U. S. A.

704—F., 1887.

WAR DEPARTMENT,

Quartermaster General's Office.

Specifications for Cords and Bands for Helmets.

To be made of worsted No. 26, and "machined cord," dyed a fast color to shade of standard sample.

The bands are loop-plaited, fastened to the scroll-rings, and festooned on front and back of helmet, the festoons reaching in front to the upper edge of chin-strap, and approaching the lower edge of back within two (2) inches.

The loop-plaiting is about one (1) inch wide, and ends under the scrolls on the left side in a tassel of sixty (60) to seventy (70) fringes one and three-fourths (1¾) inches long. Through the braided head, about three-fourths (¾) inch diameter, passes the continuation of the bands in the form of two cords, each five (5) feet eight (8) inches long, with two (2) slides netted over a fuller's board three-fourths (¾) inch in diameter, five-eighths (⅝) of an inch high. Three inches from the lower end the cords are fastened together by a braided knot, holding a loop about two and three-fourths (2¾) inches long. At the end of each cord is also a small braided knot, and an aiguillette, plaited flat in three strands of smaller cord, in oval shape, two and three-eighths (2⅜) inches long, two and three-fourths (2¾) inches wide. From the lower end of each aiguillette is suspended another tassel of from sixty (60) to seventy (70) fringes, one and three-fourths (1¾) inches long, with braided head three-eighths of an inch high, three-fourths (¾) inch diameter.

Adopted April 5, 1887.

S. B. HOLABIRD,
Quartermaster General, U. S. A.

704—F., 1887.

160

WAR DEPARTMENT,

QUARTERMASTER GENERAL'S OFFICE.

Specifications for Dark-Blue Flannel, fine quality.

Wool.—To be pure long-staple American fleece wool of not less than three-quarters (¾) blood, free from shoddy, flocks, or other impurities.

Width.—To be fifty-four (54) inches, or six-fourths ($\frac{6}{4}$) of a yard wide.

Threads.—To contain not less than sixty-eight (68) threads of warp and seventy-two (72) threads of filling in each square inch.

Weight.—To weigh not less than thirteen (13) ounces to the linear yard.

Strength.—To be capable of sustaining a strain of not less than twenty-seven (27) pounds to the inch of warp, and twenty-five (25) pounds to the inch of filling.

Color.—To be of same shade of dark-blue as the standard sample, and to be dyed in the wool with pure indigo, of best quality (unless otherwise authorized in writing by the contracting officer).

Finish.—To be equal in all respects to the standard sample.

Adopted April 16, 1887.

S. B. HOLABIRD,
Quartermaster General, U. S. A.

761—F., 1887.

161

WAR DEPARTMENT,

QUARTERMASTER GENERAL'S OFFICE.

Specifications for Trumpet-Cords and Tassels.

Material.—Cord : U. S. Gauge No. 5, made on 16 Carrier machine, one end of No. 18 four-fold Genappe, best quality, filling cotton. Tassel : Hard wood-mold, two (2) inches, covered on 48 Carrier machine, one end No. 18 four-fold Genappe. Skirt : Seven ends No. 26 two-fold worsted, single twist, ⅜ blood stock, three (3) inches deep, about 80 bullions to the tassel.

Gimp.—Brass wire and cotton spun, with one end No. 18 four-fold Genappe, six rows.

Length.—Length of cord to be twenty-one (21) feet.

Dyeing.—To be fast color.

Colors.—To be white for Infantry, scarlet for Artillery, and yellow for Cavalry, conforming in shade to that of the standard samples.

Adopted June 1, 1887.

S. B. HOLABIRD,
Quartermaster General, U. S. A.

1102—F., 1887.

CORD AND TASSELS

TRUMPET.

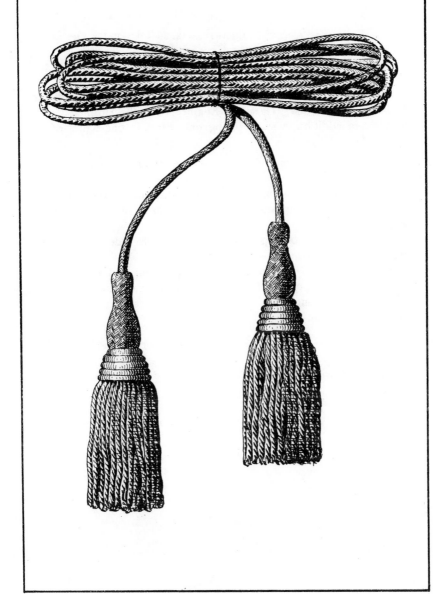

WAR DEPARTMENT,

QUARTERMASTER GENERAL'S OFFICE.

Specifications for Trousers Stripes.

Materials.—To be of facing-cloth, of the same color as facings for Uniform Dress Coats. Those for Engineers and the Hospital Corps to have, in addition, a white piping on each side one-eighth of an inch wide.

Dimensions.—For non-commissioned staff, one and one-quarter ($1\frac{1}{4}$) inches wide.

For Sergeants and Acting Hospital Stewards, one (1) inch wide.

For Coporals and Privates of the Hospital Corps, one-half ($\frac{1}{2}$) inch wide.

For Musicians, two stripes, one-half ($\frac{1}{2}$) inch wide, placed one-quarter ($\frac{1}{4}$) inch apart.

All stripes to be cut forty-five (45) inches long, and wide enough to be turned in one-quarter ($\frac{1}{4}$) of an inch on either side.

To be worn along the outer seam of the trousers, the rear edge following the seam.

Adopted August 24, 1887, in lieu of specifications of March 24, 1885, which are hereby canceled.

The specifications for Linen Webbing, adopted March 24, 1886, are also canceled.

S. B. HOLABIRD,
Quartermaster General, ·U. S. A.

1859—F., 1887.
1802—F., 1887.

Specifications for Blouses.

Material.—Dark-blue wool flannel, Army standard; blue twilled mixed flannel lining for body, and unbleached muslin lining for sleeves.

Pattern.—To be single-breasted sack coat with falling collar, and having five (5) regulation buttons, large, in front from neck to waist, and three (3) regulation buttons, small, on the cuff of each sleeve. To have three (3) outside pockets, one (1) on each side of skirt, and one (1) on the left breast, and one (1) inside pocket on the right breast.

Workmanship.—To be cut, made, and finished in accordance with the standard samples adopted this date.

MEASUREMENTS.

Sizes.	Length of Blouse.	Length of Sleeves.	Width at Hand.	Size of Neck.	Width of Collar.	Width of Back.	Size of Armhole.	Size of Breast.	Size of Waist.
					INCHES.				
1	27	31	12	16	3	7	16	34	32
2	27½	31½	12	16½	3	7½	17	35	33
3	28	32½	12	17	3	7¾	18	36	34
4	29	33	12	18	3½	8	19	38	36
5	30¼	34	12½	19	3½	8	20	40	38
6	30½	34½	13	19½	3½	8¼	21	42	40

Adopted October 20, 1887, *in lieu of specifications of March* 12, 1886, *which are hereby canceled.*

S. B. HOLABIRD,

Quartermaster General, U. S. A.

2438—F., 1887.

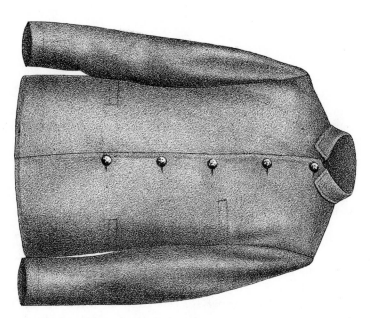

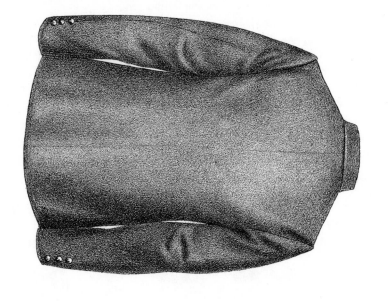

BLOUSE.

167

WAR DEPARTMENT,

QUARTERMASTER GENERAL'S OFFICE.

Specifications for Hospital Flags.

Material.—To be of the best quality of U. S. Standard Bunting.

Pattern.—For General Hospitals: Body to be white, 9 feet fly by 5 feet hoist, with a red Geneva cross in the center 4 feet high and 4 feet wide; arms of cross to be 16 inches wide.

For Post and Field Hospitals: Body to be white, 6 feet fly and 4 feet hoist, with a red Geneva cross in the center 3 feet high and 3 feet wide; arms of cross to be 12 inches wide.

For Ambulances and Guidons to mark the way to Field Hospitals: Body to be white, 28 inches fly by 16 inches hoist, with a red Geneva cross in the center 12 inches high and 12 inches wide; arms of cross to be 4 inches wide.

The heading for flags for General Hospitals and Post and Field Hospitals to be of stout 8-ounce Cotton Duck, 4 inches wide, doubled to the flag, making it 2 inches wide when completed, and to have a piece of stout 1½-inch webbing through it extending the whole width of the flag. A galvanized iron staple and ring to be placed at each end of the flag heading, fastened with 3 copper rivets.

The flag for Ambulances and Guidons to mark the way to Field Hospitals to have a 2-inch heading of same material as the flag, lined with heavy muslin for a pike to pass through.

The pike is to be of ash, finished at the top with a wooden cone and at the foot with a brass-pointed ferrule. Total length about 4 feet 5 inches.

Workmanship and Finish.—To conform in all respects to the sealed standard sample.

Adopted January 23, 1888.

S. B. HOLABIRD,
Quartermaster General, U. S. A.

3025—F., 1887.

HOSPITAL FLAGS.

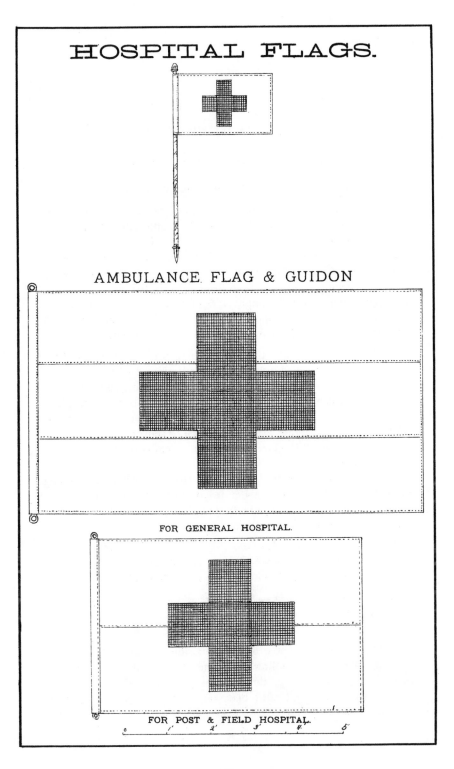

AMBULANCE. FLAG & GUIDON

FOR GENERAL HOSPITAL.

FOR POST & FIELD HOSPITAL.

Specifications for Gold Lace Chevrons.

Lace.—To be made of gold lace of Army standard.

Cloths.—The cloth forming the groundwork for arms, arcs, and ties of chevrons to be of facing cloth (conforming to published specifications) of the same color as the facings of the uniform coat.

The cloth forming the groundwork for chevron devices to be the same as that of the uniform coat. To be cut in shape of a quadrant of a circle having a radius of from five (5) to six (6) inches (as size of device may require), the straight sides of pieces to be neatly stitched to the under side of the upper edge of cloth of arms, the nap of the cloth to run downward when the chevron is on the sleeve.

Bars and Arms.—The bars of the chevrons to be a single width of lace, to be neatly joined at the angles and stitched with gold-colored silk upon the facing cloth, on each border of the lace, and also at the outer ends, which are to be turned under. The bars to be placed about one-eighth (⅛) of an inch apart, and a bordering of the facing cloth of about one eighth (⅛) of one inch to show on all sides.

The chevrons for Engineers to have a stitching of white silk upon each side of the lace bars.

The arms of the chevron bars to be six (6) to seven (7) inches long, to be the arcs of a circle of about twenty-five (25) inches radius, and to meet at an angle of about ninety-six (96) degrees ; distance between extreme outer ends, about nine (9) inches.

Design for Chevrons—Sergeant Major.—Three bars and an arc of three bars. The upper edge of outer bar of arc to be the arc of a circle of about seven and one-fourth (7¼) inches radius.

Quartermaster Sergeant.—Three bars and a tie of three bars. The upper bar of tie to extend horizontally from the extreme outer end of one arm of the chevron to that of the other.

Saddler Sergeant.—Three bars and a saddler's round knife; handle upward. Knife of the following dimensions: handle one and three-fourths (1¾) inches long, three-fourths (¾) inch wide near top, five-eighths (⅝) inch near blade ; blade one and one-eighth (1⅛) inches deep in center; from point to point of blade, three and one-fourth

($3\frac{1}{4}$) inches; center of edge one and one-fourth ($1\frac{1}{4}$) inches above inner angle of chevron. Lace of handle to run vertically, of ferrule about horizontally, and of blade to be crimped to shape of same.

Chief Trumpeter.—Three bars and an arc of one bar, with bugle of pattern worn on cap, about one and one-half ($1\frac{1}{2}$) inches above inner angle of chevron. The upper edge of bar of arc to be the arc of a circle of about seven and one-fourth ($7\frac{1}{4}$) inches radius. Bugle to be of form, dimensions, and finish of the standard sample chevron.

Principal Musician.—Three bars and a bugle. The bugle to be the same as for Chief Trumpeter chevrons.

Ordnance Sergeants.—Three bars and an outlined star of lace. Lower point of star to be about one (1) inch above inner angle of chevron. Star to be of dimensions and finish of the standard sample chevron.

Post Quartermaster Sergeant.—Three bars and a crossed key and pen. The latter device to be embroidered on gold bullion. The key and pen to cross about two and one-half ($2\frac{1}{2}$) inches above the inner angle of the chevron, and to be of form, dimensions, and finish of standard sample chevron.

Commissary Sergeant.—Three bars and a crescent (points front). Distance from point to point of crescent two (2) inches, width in center three-fourths ($\frac{3}{4}$) of one inch, center of lower edge to be about one and three-fourths ($1\frac{3}{4}$) inches above inner angle of chevron.

Hospital Steward.—Three bars and an arc of one bar with a red cross placed about one and seven-eighths ($1\frac{7}{8}$) inches above inner angle of chevron. The upper edge of bar of arc to be the arc of a circle of about seven and one-fourth ($7\frac{1}{4}$) inches radius. Cross to be of form, dimensions, and finish of standard sample chevron.

Acting Hospital Steward.—Same as for Hospital Steward, omitting the arc.

1st Sergeants.—Three bars and an outlined lozenge, having sides about one-fourth ($\frac{1}{4}$) of an inch wide. Lozenge about two and one-half ($2\frac{1}{2}$) inches long and two (2) inches wide, placed lengthwise, about one and one-fourth ($1\frac{1}{4}$) inches above inner angle of chevron.

Sergeants.—Three bars.

Regimental and Batallion Color Sergeant.—Three bars and a sphere one-fourth ($\frac{1}{4}$) of an inch wide, and one and one-fourth ($1\frac{1}{4}$) inches in outside diameter, and placed one and three-fourths ($1\frac{3}{4}$) inches above inner angle of chevron.

Corporal.—Two bars.

To indicate service.—A single width of lace neatly stitched upon a piece of cloth of color of uniform coat, the ends of lace to be turned under; a bordering of the cloth one-eighth (⅛) of an inch wide to appear on all sides. Length of chevron, about nine and one-fourth (9¼) inches.

To indicate service in war.—The same as above, except that facing cloth of the color of the facings of the particular arm of service will be substituted for the other cloth.

Workmanship.—To be in accordance with the standard samples adopted this day.

Adopted January 27, 1888, *in lieu of specifications of August* 25, 1885, *which are hereby canceled.*

S. B. HOLABIRD,
Quartermaster General, U. S. A.

165—F., 1888.

CHEVRONS.

GOLD LACE.

SERGEANT MAJOR.

FIRST SERGEANT.

CHEVRONS.

GOLD LACE.

REGIMENTAL AND BATTALION COLOR SERGEANT

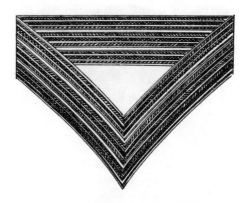

QUARTERMASTER SERGEANT.

CHEVRONS.
GOLD LACE.

SADDLER SERGEANT.

POST QUARTERMASTER SERGEANT.

CHEVRONS.

GOLD LACE.

CHIEF TRUMPETER.

0   3"   6"

CHEVRONS.

GOLD LACE.

PRINCIPAL MUSICIAN.

SERGEANT.

CHEVRONS.

GOLD LACE.

ORDNANCE SERGEANT.

CORPORAL.

CHEVRONS.

GOLD LACE.

HOSPITAL STEWARD.

ACTING HOSPITAL STEWARD.

CHEVRONS.

GOLD LACE.

COMMISSARY SERGEANT.

SERVICE PEACE.

SERVICE WAR.

WAR DEPARTMENT,
QUARTERMASTER GENERAL'S OFFICE.

Specifications for Uniform Dress-Coats.

Material.—Dark-blue cloth, Army standard. That for non-commissioned officers to be of finer quality than for privates. Linings: for body and sleeves, corset jeans; for skirt, black Italian cloth; regulation brass buttons.

Pattern and Dimensions—For Foot Troops.—Single-breasted, dark-blue frock coat, according to standard sample; nine (9) buttons in front; standing collar, cut square, to hook in front; cloth facings and pipings, of color for the various arms of service on collar, cuff, and back of skirt, according to pattern; shoulder-straps of facing-cloth let into seam at point of shoulder, and to button at collar with one (1) button; inside pocket in left breast, opening perpendicularly.

For Mounted Troops.—To be similar to the above, except that the skirt be three (3) inches shorter, and be slashed and piped at sides to within about three (3) inches of the waist, and the back facing to be according to standard sample.

For Musicians.—To be the same as above, with the addition of the breast facings (according to pattern) of one-fourth (¼) inch worsted braid, of proper color for the arm of service.

For Enlisted Men of the Staff Corps.—To be the same as the above, except that the piping be white for all corps, and the edges of all facings and straps be piped with white cloth, according to sample. Coat for acting hospital steward to have in addition a red cross on each side of the collar in front.

MEASUREMENTS FOR UNIFORM DRESS-COATS, FOOT.

SIZES.	1	2	3	4	5	6
	Inches.	*Inches.*	*Inches.*	*Inches.*	*Inches.*	*Inches.*
From collar seam to waist	18	18½	19¼	19½	20¼	20¾
Full length of coat	32	32½	33¼	33½	34¼	34¾
" " sleeve	31	31¾	32½	34	35	35½
Width of back	7	7¼	7¾	8	8¼	8⅜
Collar at neck	15¼	15¾	16	17	17½	18⅜
Height of collar, front	1	1	1	1	1	1
" " back	1¼	1¼	1¼	1¼	1¼	1¼
Width of sleeve at hand	5½	5½	6	6¼	6¼	6½
Breast measure	35	36½	38	40	41	43
Waist measure	32	34	36	38	39	41

MEASUREMENTS FOR UNIFORM DRESS-COATS, MOUNTED.

SIZES.	1	2	3	4	5	6
	Inches.	Inches.	Inches.	Inches.	Inches.	Inches.
From collar seam to waist	17½	18	18¾	19	19¾	20¼
Full length of coat	28½	29	29¾	30	30¾	31¼
" " sleeve	31	31¾	32½	34	35	35½
Width of back	7	7¼	7¾	8	8¼	8⅜
Collar at neck	15¼	15¾	16	17	17½	18⅜
Height of collar, front	1	1	1	1	1	1
" " back	1¼	1¼	1¼	1¼	1¼	1¼
Width of sleeve at hand	5½	5½	6	6¼	6¼	6½
Breast measure	35	36½	38	40	41	43
Waist measure	32	34	36	38	39	41

Adopted January 27, 1888, *in lieu of those of March* 5, 1885, *which are hereby canceled.*

S. B. HOLABIRD,
Quartermaster General, U. S. A.

165—F., 1888.

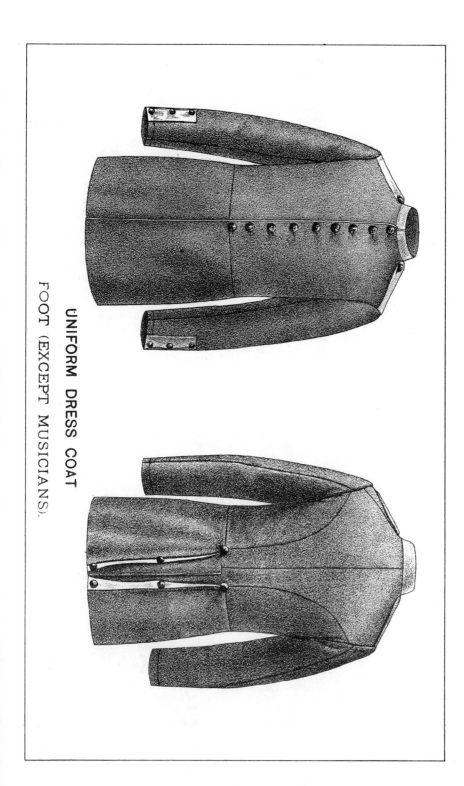

UNIFORM DRESS COAT

FOOT (EXCEPT MUSICIANS).

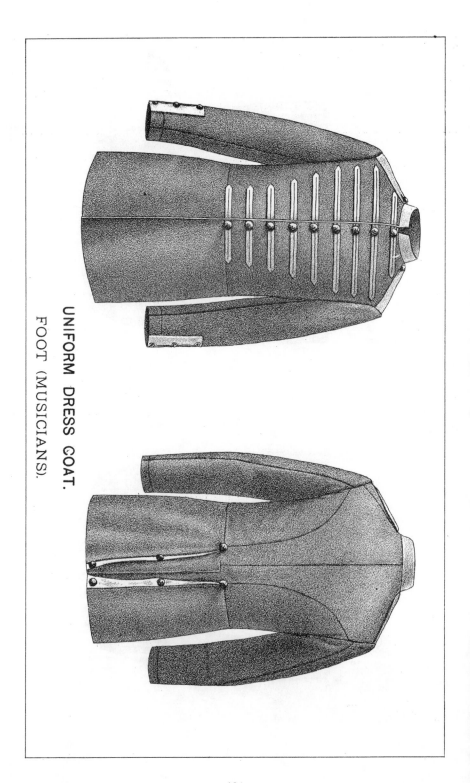

UNIFORM DRESS COAT.

FOOT (MUSICIANS).

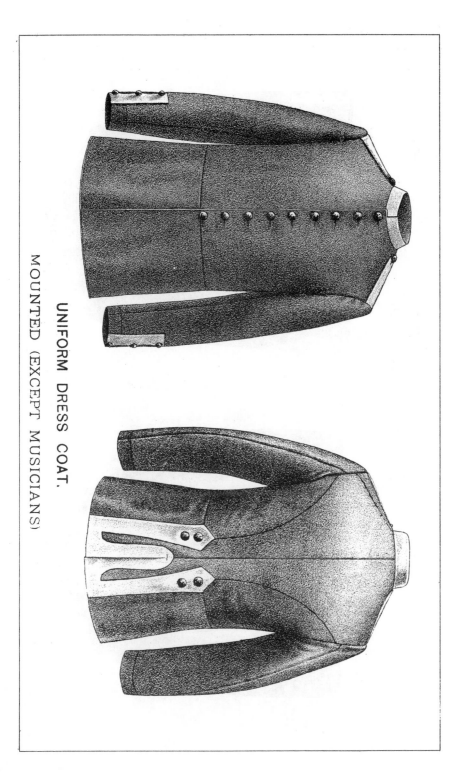

UNIFORM DRESS COAT.

MOUNTED (EXCEPT MUSICIANS)

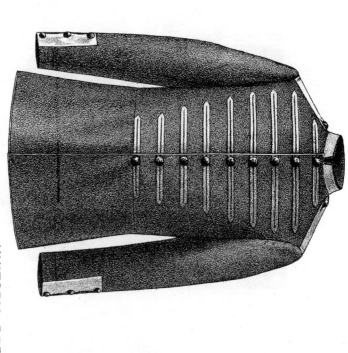

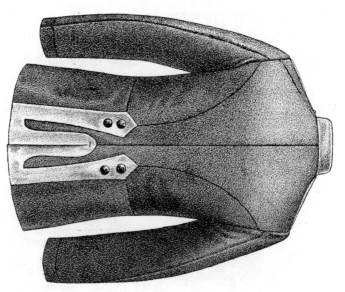

UNIFORM DRESS COAT.

MOUNTED (MUSICIANS).

WAR DEPARTMENT,

Quartermaster General's Office.

Specifications for Trowsers.

Material.—Dark-blue cloth for enlisted men of the Hospital Corps, for all others sky-blue kersey. The cloth and kersey for non-commissioned officers to be of finer quality than for privates.

For Foot Troops.—To be cut and made in accordance with the standard patterns and samples approved January 16, 1884. To have side pockets and a hip pocket on the right side. The bottoms to be lined with canvas.

For Mounted Troops.—To be similar to those for foot-men, with the addition of a reinforce or saddle-piece of the same material on seat and legs. Four buttons at bottom of each leg, two (2) on each side for straps.

SIZE.	Waist, Inches.	Seat, Inches.	Crotch, Inches.	Outside Seam, Inches.	Inside Seam, Inches.	Knee, Inches.	Bottom, Inches.
1	31	36	23	41	31	17½	19
2	32	36	23	40	30	17½	19
3	32	37	23	43	33	17¾	19¼
4	32	38	24	42	32	18	19¾
5	33	38	24	41¼	31	18¼	19¾
6	33	39	24	44½	34	18¼	19¾
7	34	39	25	42½	32	18½	20¼
8	34	40	25½	45½	35	18½	20¼
9	36	41	26	42¾	32	19	20½
10	36	41	26	44	33	19	20½
11	38	43	26	45	34	19½	21
12	40	44	26½	44¼	33	19½	21

Adopted January 27, 1888, in lieu of specifications of January 16, 1884, which are hereby canceled.

S. B. HOLABIRD,
Quartermaster General, U. S. A.

265—F., 1888.

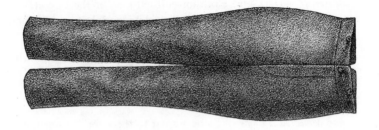

TROUSERS.

FOOT.

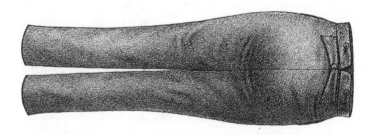

188

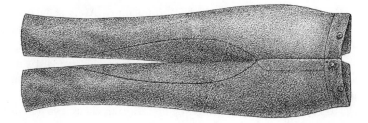

TROUSERS.

MOUNTED.

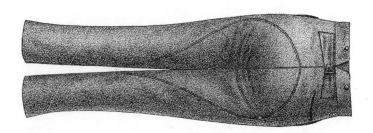

189

WAR DEPARTMENT,
QUARTERMASTER GENERAL'S OFFICE.

Specifications for Drawers.

Material.—To be unbleached Canton flannel, Army standard.

Drawers.—To be made without waistbands, in lieu of which a reinforcing piece will be placed around the top, and extend down the front, fashioned in like manner and size as on the standard samples, buttoning with two (2) buttons about two and one-half (2½) inches apart.

To have facings, or reinforcing pieces, each about two (2) inches wide, double stitched on as in standard, extending from point of reinforcing at the waist in front to within about ten (10) inches of the opening at back of waist; this opening to be four and one-half (4½) inches long, with four (4) worked eyelet holes and lacing strings of three-quarter (¾) inch white cotton tape.

To have opening at bottom of each leg five (5) inches long, and bottom bands one (1) inch wide, with one (1) button and one (1) button-hole on each leg.

The openings in back of waist and in legs to be neatly faced with Canton flannel about one (1) inch wide; all openings to be secured by button-hole stitch.

DIMENSIONS OF EACH SIZE TO BE AS FOLLOWS:

	No. 1.	No. 2.	No. 3.	No. 4.	No. 5.
	Inches.	*Inches.*	*Inches.*	*Inches.*	*Inches.*
Length of side seam	39	40½	41½	43	45
Length of leg seam	29	30	31	32	33
Waist	31	32	34	36	38

Adopted February 6, 1888, *in lieu of specifications of May* 25, 1883, *which are hereby canceled.*

S. B. HOLABIRD,
Quartermaster General, U. S. A.

298—F., 1888.

190

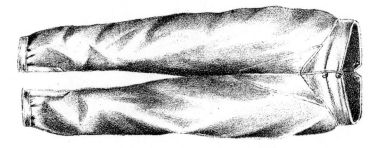

DRAWERS.

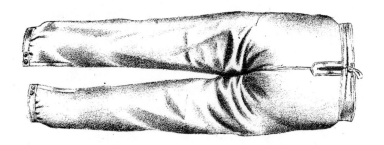

WAR DEPARTMENT,

QUARTERMASTER GENERAL'S OFFICE.

Specifications for Corset Jeans.

To be twenty-seven (27) inches wide when finished. The color to be a light drab, as per standard sample. To be soft finished.

To contain not less than one hundred and twelve (112) threads to the inch in the warp, and sixty-four (64) threads to the inch in the filling.

To weigh not less than three and fifty-six one hundredths $(3\frac{56}{100})$ ounces to the yard, or four and one-half $(4\frac{1}{2})$ yards to the pound.

To be capable of sustaining a strain of sixty (60) pounds to the inch of warp, and twenty-five (25) pounds to the inch of filling.

Adopted February 25, 1888.

S. B. HOLABIRD,
Quartermaster General, U. S. A.

482—F., 1888.

WAR DEPARTMENT,

QUARTERMASTER GENERAL'S OFFICE.

Specifications for Uniform Coat Buttons (Staff).

Size.—To be of two (2) sizes, designated as large and small. The large size to be thirty-six (36) lignes and the small size twenty-three (23) lignes.

Shell.—The shell of the large size buttons to be made from low brass, number twenty-six (26) gauge. The small size to be of same metal, number twenty-eight (28) gauge.

Rims.—The rims of both large and small size to be made from low brass, number thirty-three (33) gauge.

Backs.—The backs of both large and small size to be of soldering brass, number twenty-six (26) gauge.

Eyes.—The eye of the large size buttons to be of copper wire, number thirteen (13) gauge, and the small size of same wire, number fifteen (15) gauge.

Gilding.—The gilding to be done by fire process, and shell and rim to be so treated that all the gold shall be on the outside. The weight of gold on each gross of shells, large size, to be not less than four-fifths ($\frac{4}{5}$) of a pennyweight. The weight of gold on each gross of rims, large size, to be not less than one-fifth ($\frac{1}{5}$) of a pennyweight. The weight of gold on each gross of shells, small size, to be not less than two-fifths ($\frac{2}{5}$) of a pennyweight. The weight of gold on each gross of rims, small size, to be not less than one-tenth ($\frac{1}{10}$) of a pennyweight.

Burnishing.—The burnishing to be done in the best manner known to the trade.

Stamping.—The stamping to be done with sharp, bright dies, free from any imperfections.

Solder.—The eye to be soldered into the back of the button with best quality spelter solder, and no backs to be used that show an abrasion around the eye.

Closing.—The shell, back, and rim to be joined together with a thin piece of cardboard between, thus making a substantial and perfect joint.

Color.—To conform to standard samples.

Acid Test.—To stand an acid test equal to standard samples.

Packing.—The buttons to be put up in gross boxes on cards of two (2) dozen each. Each card to be protected by two (2) thicknesses of tissue paper.

The gauge mentioned in these specifications is known as Brown & Sharp's Standard Metal Gauge.

Adopted March 10, 1888.

S. B. HOLABIRD,
Quartermaster General, U. S. A.

574—F., 1888.

BUTTONS,
UNIFORM COAT.
STAFF.

SMALL.

LARGE.

Specifications for Conical Wall Tents.

Material.—Body of tent to be made of standard twelve (12) ounce cotton duck, and the sod cloth of standard eight (8) ounce cotton duck, twenty-eight and one-half (28½) inches wide. Eave lines of six (6) thread manila line (large), and foot lines of nine (9) thread manila line.

Work.—To be made in a workmanlike manner with not less than two and one-half (2½) stitches of equal length to the inch, made with a double thread of five-fold cotton twine well waxed. The seams to be not less than one (1) inch in width and no slack taken in them.

Form and Dimensions.—The roof to be in the form of a frustum of a cone, sixteen (16) feet five (5) inches in diameter at the base, eighteen (18) inches in diameter at the top. Wall to be three (3) feet high. Height, when pitched, to top of roof ten (10) feet. Eaves to be two (2) inches wide, and tabling at bottom two and one-half (2½) inches wide. The angle from the top to the eave, ten feet one and one-quarter (10′ 1¼″) inches.

Top.—The top opening at the top to be formed with a galvanized-iron ring eighteen (18) inches in diameter, over which the duck shall be firmly stitched and reinforced down the roof to a depth of eight and one-half (8½) inches. Six (6) three-quarter (¾) inch grommet holes around the top, equal distances just below the ring, to be reinforced with leather in which to hook the chains which support the tent on the pole.

Plate and Chains.—The plate to be four (4) inches in diameter and one-quarter (¼) inch in thickness, with six (6) three-eighths (⅜) inch holes around the edge at equal distances and countersunk, and a five-eighth (⅝) inch hole in the center. Chains, six (6) in number, to be fourteen (14) inches long, including hook, made of machine chain No. 1. All to be of galvanized iron.

Door.—Doorway to be seven (7) feet high measured along the seam, thirteen and one-quarter (13¼) inches wide at top, twenty-five and one-quarter (25¼) inches at bottom. The door of two equal pieces in area to the doorway, and joined at opposite sides of the same so as to lap and form double thickness when closed. Tabling on edge to be two (2) inches when finished. To have an interlining of No. 4 canvas, four (4) inches long and one and one-half (1½) inches wide, as stays for the grommets, six (6) in number.

Door Fastenings.—To consist of five (5) No. 5 conical pointed brass grommets on each side, placed at equal distances of sixteen (16) inches from the top of door to the eave, and eighteen (18) inches from the eave down on the wall, holes to be worked on the seams the same distance, with five-eighths (⅝) inch galvanized-iron rings; door lines of one-quarter (¼) inch white cotton rope forty (40) inches long and whipped on both ends, to be seized in the middle with a knot on each side of the hole that the door may be tied either inside or outside. Two (2) five-eighths (⅝) inch holes worked eight (8) inches above the lip of the door, with two (2) one-quarter (¼) inch cotton lines one (1) foot long in the clear, with a "Mathew Walker" knot on one end and properly whipped on the other end; one (1) hole one-half (½) inch worked on each side at the bottom, with one (1) six (6) thread manila line three (3) feet long for door line. Four (4) lines twenty-four (24) inches long, made of No. 3 gilling line, placed on the eave on the inside of the tent on both sides of the door, for tying the doors back when open.

Sod Cloth.—The sod cloth to be eight and three-quarter (8¾) inches wide in the clear, and to extend around the inside of the tent from door to door.

Grommet Holes.—Twenty-four (24) in number, worked on the seams of the foot of the tent over three-quarter (¾) inch galvanized malleable-iron rings, and twenty-four (24) one-half (½) inch holes to be worked on the seams of the eaves over galvanized-iron rings, the holes to be worked with four (4) thread five-fold cotton twine well waxed.

Hood.—Conical hood open at side, and faced at the bottom with ten (10) ounce duck, two (2) inches wide, when finished, and having hole in apex, worked over seven-eighth (⅞) inch galvanized-iron ring, to admit spindle of pole; to extend down the roof at least six (6) inches below the top, with five (5) one-half (½) inch holes worked over galvanized-iron rings at the bottom for lines, which are to be made of six (6) thread manila line sixteen (16) feet long and spliced in the holes and properly whipped on the end.

Eave Lines.—Twenty-four (24) in number, to be six (6) thread manila line (large), and to be six (6) feet six (6) inches long, with eye four (4) inches spliced on one end and properly whipped on the other. To be furnished with a metallic slip No. 3.

Foot Lines.—Twenty-four (24) in number, to be four (4) inches long in the clear, and to be in the form of a loop passing through a single grommet hole, stopped by a "Mathew Walker" knot.

Wall Lines.—Twenty-four (24) in number, to be two (2) feet long, to be made of No. 3 gilling line whipped at both ends, and placed under the eaves on the seams for tying the wall up.

To be like and equal in all respects to the standard sample. No "butts" or pieces in any of the cloths, and no brands on the outside.

Adopted August 9, 1888, in lieu of specifications of May 23, 1884, which are hereby canceled.

C. G. SAWTELLE,
Deputy Quartermaster General, U. S. A., in charge.

2127—F., 1888.

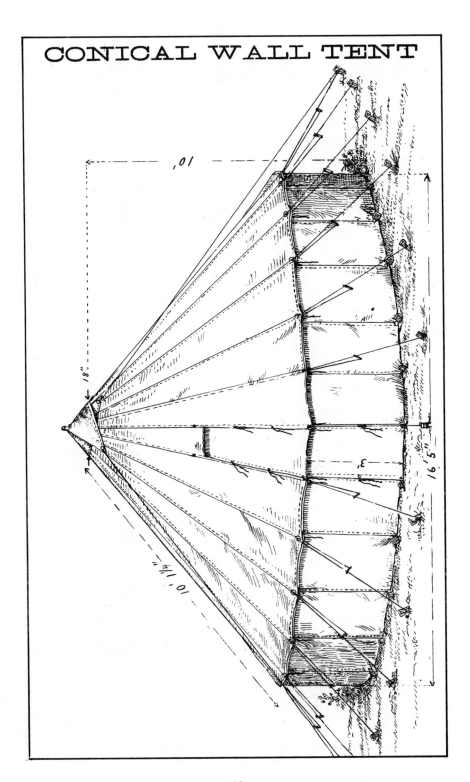

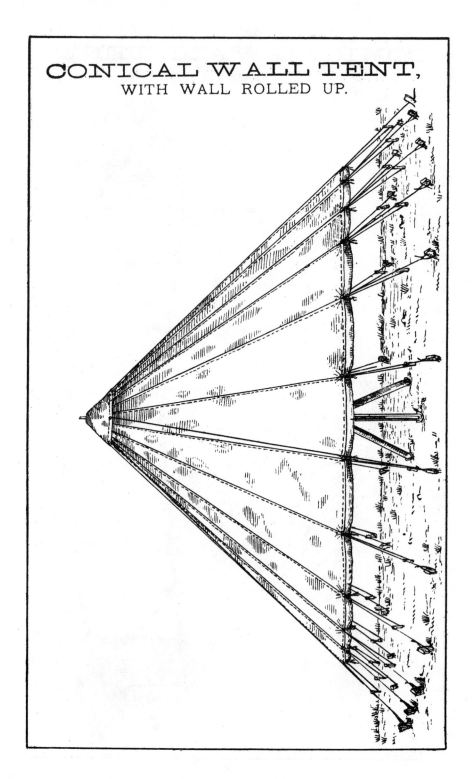

CONICAL WALL TENT,
WITH WALL ROLLED UP.

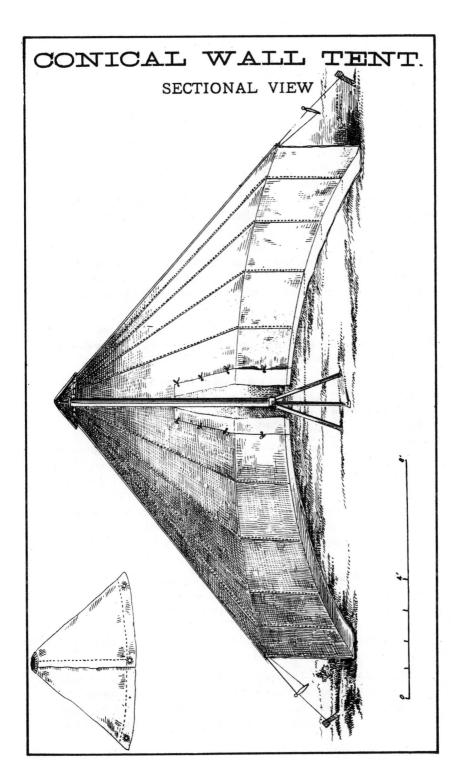

CONICAL WALL TENT.

SECTIONAL VIEW

Specifications for Hospital Tents.

Dimensions.—Dimensions when finished: Height, when pitched, eleven (11) feet; length of ridge, fourteen (14) feet; width, when pitched, fourteen (14) feet six (6) inches; height of wall, when pitched, four (4) feet (6) inches; wall eaves, three (3) inches in width; height of door, when pitched, eight (8) feet nine (9) inches; width of door, when pitched, eighteen (18) inches at bottom and ten (10) inches at top; from top of ridge to wall, nine (9) feet ten (10) inches.

Material.—To be made of cotton duck twenty-eight and one-half (28½) inches wide, clear of all imperfection, and weighing twelve (12) ounces to the linear yard.

Work.—To be made in a workmanlike manner, with not less than two and one-half (2½) stitches of equal length to the inch, made with double thread of five-fold cotton twine well waxed. The seams not less than one (1) inch in width, and no slack taken in them.

Grommets—Grommets made with malleable-iron rings, galvanized, must be worked in all the holes, and be well made with four-thread five-fold cotton twine well waxed. Sizes of grommets: For eaves, one-half (½) inch rings; for foot-stops, three-quarter (¾) inch rings, and for ridge, seven-eighth (⅞) inch rings, the latter to be worked so that the center will measure two and one-fourth (2¼) inches from edge of roof, so as to be in correct position to receive spindle of upright poles.

Door and Stay Pieces.—Door and stay pieces to be of the same material as the tent. The stay pieces on end triangular in shape, fourteen (14) inches on base and perpendicular, and on the ridge one (1) foot square; those at corners of tent at angle of roof and wall, to be eight (8) inches wide, let into the tabling at the eaves, and extending eight (8) inches up the roof and eight (8) inches down the wall.

Extension Cloth.—The extension cloth, thirteen (13) inches wide in the clear, to be of the same material as the tent, and stitched to it with two (2) rows of flat stitching, four (4) inches back from the edge of the tent. This extension cloth should be cut four (4) inches longer than the body of the tent and the slack taken in. Grommets of the required sizes to be worked in proper places for upright spindle and for eave lines.

Sod Cloth.—The sod cloth to be of eight (8) ounce cotton duck, twelve (12) inches in width in the clear from the tabling, and underlying it two and one-quarter (2¼) inches, and to extend from door to door around all sides of the tent.

Tabling.—The tabling on foot of tent, when finished, to be two and one-half (2½) inches in width.

Ventilator.—An aperture five (5) inches wide and ten (10) inches long, one (1) in the front and one (1) in the back end of the tent, placed six (6) inches from the top and two (2) inches from the center on the right side of each end. The aperture to be reinforced with ten (10) ounce cotton duck, and to have the edges turned in and stitched all around. A flap or curtain on the inside eight (8) inches wide and fourteen (14) inches long, finished; to be made of two (2) ply eight (8) ounce cotton duck, stitched around the edges; to have one (1) "No. 2" sheet-brass grommet placed at the top for the purpose of tying it up to close the opening; strings made of "No. 3" gilling line to be used for tying the curtain in place.

Guy Lines.—Two (2) guy lines of twelve-thread manila line, soft and pliable, each thirty (30) feet long in the clear, and furnished with "No. 1" metallic slips.

Eave Lines.—Eave lines, fourteen (14) in number, to be of nine-thread manila line (large), and to be ten (10) feet six (6) inches long in the clear, with an eye four (4) inches long, spliced on one end, the other end properly whipped, and each line furnished with a metallic slip, "No. 3," Army standard.

Door Lines.—Door lines of six-thread manila line, three (3) feet long in the clear.

Wall Lines.—Twenty-six (26) in number, to be two (2) feet long, to be made of "No. 3" gilling line, whipped at both ends and placed under the eaves on the seams for tying the wall up.

Door Fastenings.—Door fastenings, as shown in sample tent, to consist of four (4) double door strings of one-fourth (¼) inch cotton rope one (1) foot long, on each side, passing through the door seam and secured by a "Mathew Walker" knot. Brass grommets, "No. 5," conical points, to be in corresponding positions on edge of door piece in which to tie the door cords. A two (2) inch tabling to be made on edge of door.

Foot-stops.—Foot-stops, twenty-six (26) in number, to be loops four (4) inches long in the clear, of nine-thread manila line, both ends passing through a single grommet worked in the tabling at seams, and to be held by what is known as the "Mathew Walker" knot. Ends to be whipped with cotton twine well waxed.

The tabling at bottom, the sod cloth, and the foot-stops to be so arranged that the sod cloth falls inside and the foot-stops outside the tent.

All lines to be well whipped one (1) inch from their ends with waxed twine, and properly knotted.

To be like and equal in all respects to the standard sample. No "butts" or pieces in any of the cloths, and no brands on the outside.

Adopted August 30, 1888, *in lieu of specifications of February* 18, 1884, *which are hereby canceled.*

B. C. CARD,
Deputy Quartermaster General, U. S. A., in charge.
2278—F., 1888.

This tent requires 18 pins 26 inches and 28 pins 16 inches.

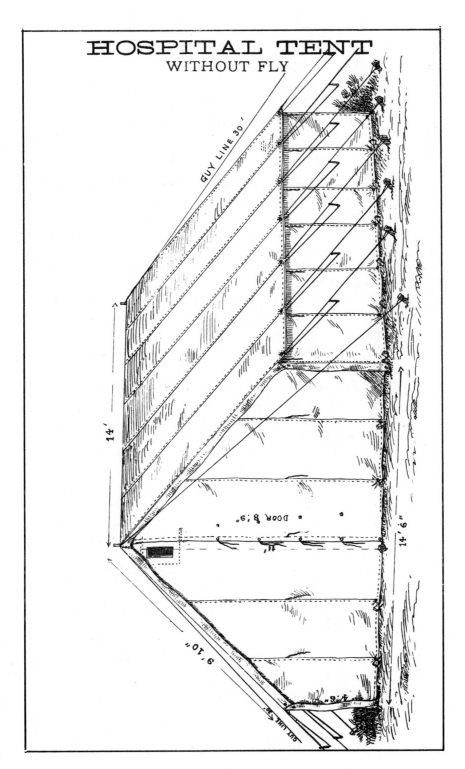

HOSPITAL TENT
WITHOUT FLY

205

WAR DEPARTMENT,

QUARTERMASTER GENERAL'S OFFICE.

Specifications for Hospital Tent Flies.

Material.—To be made of cotton duck, twenty-eight and one-half (28½) inches wide, clear of all imperfections, and weighing ten (10) ounces to the linear yard.

Dimensions.—Length, when finished, twenty-one (21) feet six (6) inches; width, fourteen (14) feet.

A three (3) inch tabling to be finished on the ends and a two (2) inch tabling on sides.

Grommets.—Grommets, made over malleable-iron rings, galvanized, must be worked in all the holes, and be well made with waxed four-thread five-fold cotton twine; size of rings, for those in end tabling one-half (½) inch, for those on ridge seven-eighths (⅞) inch.

Stay Pieces.—Stay pieces at corners same material as the fly, triangular in shape, eleven (11) inches on base and perpendicular, and on the ridge one (1) foot square finished.

Eave Lines.—Eave lines, fourteen (14) in number, to be of six-thread manila line (large), ten (10) feet long in the clear, with an eye spliced on one end four (4) inches long, the other end properly whipped and furnished with a No. 3 Metallic slip of Army standard.

Work.—The fly to be made in a workmanlike manner in every respect, with not less than two and one-half (2½) stitches of equal length to the inch, made with a double thread of five-fold cotton twine well waxed. The seams not less than one (1) inch in width and no slack taken in them.

To be like and equal in all respects to the standard sample. No "butts" or pieces in any of the cloths, and no brands on the outside.

Adopted August 30, 1888, in lieu of specifications of March 12, 1879, which are hereby canceled.

B. C. CARD,
Deputy Quartermaster General, U. S. A., in charge.

2278—F., 1888.

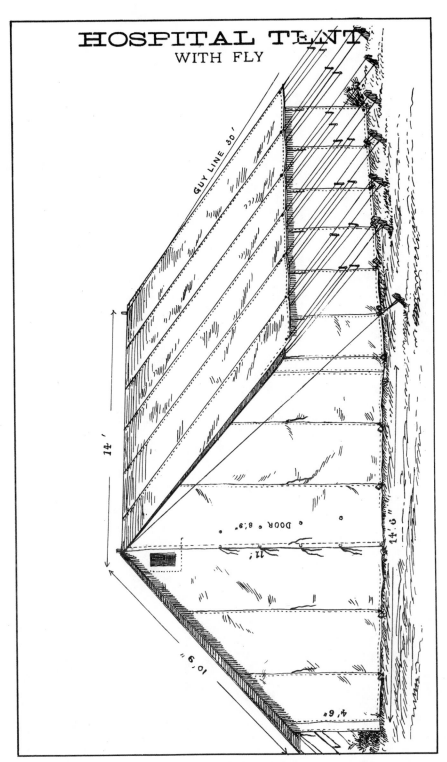

HOSPITAL TENT
WITH FLY

GUY LINE 30'

14'

DOOR 8' 9"

11'

14' 6"

10' 9"

4' 6"

207

WAR DEPARTMENT,

Quartermaster General's Office.

Specifications for Wall Tents.

Dimensions.—Height, eight (8) feet six (6) inches; length of ridge, nine (9) feet; width, eight (8) feet eleven and one-half (11½) inches; height of wall, three (3) feet nine (9) inches; wall eaves, two (2) inches wide; height of door, six (6) feet eight (8) inches; width of door, twelve (12) inches at bottom, four (4) inches at top; from top of ridge to wall, six (6) feet six (6) inches.

Material.—To be made of cotton duck twenty-eight and one-half (28½) inches wide, clear of all imperfections, and weighing twelve (12) ounces to the linear yard.

Work.—To be made in a workmanlike manner, with not less than two and one-half (2½) stitches of equal length to the inch, made with double thread of five-fold cotton twine well waxed. The seams to be not less than one (1) inch in width, and no slack taken in them.

Grommets.—Grommets made with malleable-iron rings, galvanized, must be worked in all the holes, and be well made with four-thread five-fold cotton twine well waxed. Sizes of grommets: For eaves, one-half (½) inch rings; for foot-stops, three-quarter (¾) inch rings; and for ridge, three-quarter (¾) inch rings; the latter to be worked so that the center will measure one and three-eighths (1⅜) inches from edge of roof, so as to be in correct position to receive spindle of upright poles.

Door and Stay Pieces.—Door and stay pieces to be of the same material as the tent. Stay pieces on ends and ridge of tent to be six and a half (6½) inches square; those at corners of tent, at angle of roof and wall, to be eight (8) inches wide, let into the tabling at the eaves, and extending eight (8) inches up the roof and eight (8) inches down the wall.

Back Stay.—A band or strip four (4) inches wide, of the same material as the tent, to be stitched across the back of the tent on the inside, entering into and being stitched with the corner seams at the juncture of the roof and wall.

Sod Cloth.—The sod cloth to be of eight (8) ounce cotton duck, eight and three-quarter (8¾) inches wide in the clear from the tabling, and to extend from door to door around both sides and ends of the tent.

Tabling.—The tabling on the foot of the tent, when finished, to be two and one-half (2½) inches in width.

Ventilator.—An aperture four (4) inches wide and eight (8) inches long, one (1) in the front and one (1) in the back end of the tent, placed six (6) inches from the top and two (2) inches from the center, on the right side of each end. The aperture to be reinforced with eight (8) ounce cotton duck, and to have the edges turned in and stitched all around. A flap or curtain on the inside eight (8) inches wide and fourteen (14) inches long, finished, to be made of two (2) ply eight (8) ounce cotton duck, stitched around the edges; to have one (1) "No. 1" sheet-brass grommet placed at the top for the purpose of tying it up to close the opening; strings made of "No. 2" gilling line to be used for tying the curtain in place.

Door Lines.—The door lines to be of six-thread manila line (large), three (3) feet long in the clear.

Wall Lines.—Eighteen (18) in number, to be two (2) feet long, to be made of "No. 3" gilling line, whipped at both ends and placed under the eaves on the seams, for tying the wall up.

Door Fastening.—Door fastening, as shown in sample tent, to consist of four (4) double door strings of one-fourth (¼) inch cotton rope one (1) foot long, on each side, passing through the door seam and secured by a "Mathew Walker" knot. Brass grommets, "No. 4," to be in corresponding position on edge of door piece, in which to tie the door cords. A one and one-half (1½) inch tabling to be made on the edge of door.

Foot-stops.—Foot-stops, seventeen (17) in number, to be loops four (4) inches long in the clear, of nine-thread manila line, both ends passing through a single grommet, worked in the tabling at seam, and to be held by what is known as the "Mathew Walker" knot.

Eave Lines.—Eave lines, ten (10) in number, to be of six-thread manila line (large), and be eight (8) feet long in the clear, with an eye four (4) inches long, spliced on one end, and the other end properly whipped and furnished with "No. 3" metallic slip of Army standard.

The tabling at bottom, the sod cloth, and the foot-stops to be so arranged that the sod cloth falls inside and the foot-stops outside the tent.

All lines to be well whipped one (1) inch from the end with waxed twine, and properly knotted.

To be like and equal in all respects to the standard sample. No "butts" or pieces in any of the cloths, and no brands on the outside.

Adopted August 30, 1888, in lieu of specifications of February 18, 1884, which are hereby canceled.

B. C. CARD,
Deputy Quartermaster General, U. S. A., in charge.

2278—F., 1888.

This tent requires 10 tent-pins 24-inch and 18 tent-pins 16-inch.

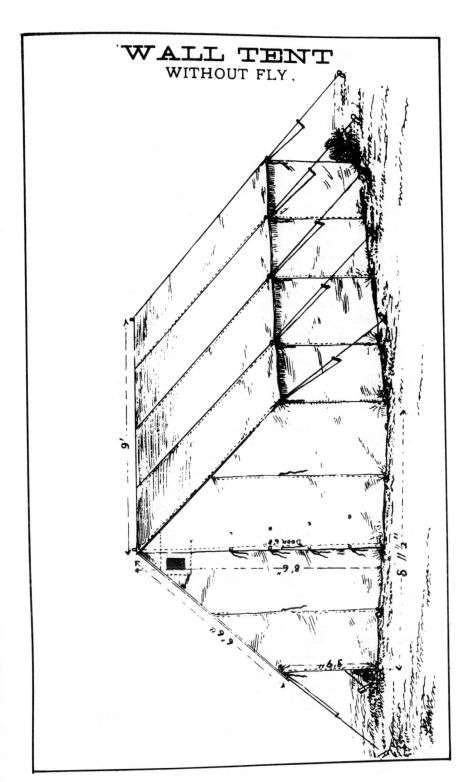

WALL TENT
WITHOUT FLY.

WAR DEPARTMENT,

QUARTERMASTER GENERAL'S OFFICE.

Specifications for Wall-Tent Flies.

Dimensions.—Length, fifteen (15) feet and six (6) inches. Width, nine (9) feet when finished.

Material.—To be made of cotton duck, twenty-eight and one-half (28½) inches wide, clear of all imperfections, and weighing (10) ounces to the linear yard.

Tabling.—A two (2) inch tabling to be worked on ends, and a one and a half (1½) inch tabling on sides.

Grommets.—Grommets made with malleable-iron rings, galvanized; to be worked in all the holes with four (4) thread five (5) fold cotton twine, well waxed. Size of grommets for eave lines, one-half (½) inch in diameter, and for upright spindle, three-fourths (¾) of an inch in diameter; the latter to be placed so as to measure one and three-eighths (1⅜) inch from their centers to edge of fly, so as to be in proper position to receive spindle.

Stay-pieces.—Stay-pieces on corners, triangular in shape, eleven (11) inches on base and perpendicular when finished, and on ridge six and one-half (6½) inches finished.

Work.—The fly is to be made in a workmanlike manner in every respect, with not less than two and a half (2½) stitches of equal length to the inch, made with double thread of five (5) fold cotton twine, well waxed.

Seams.—The seams not less than one (1) inch in width and no slack taken in them.

Eave Lines.—Eave lines, ten (10) in number, to be of six-thread manila line (large) and be seven (7) feet long in the clear, with an eye spliced on one end, four (4) inches long, the other end properly whipped, and furnished with a metallic slip No. 3, Army standard.

All lines to be well whipped one (1) inch from the end with waxed cotton twine and properly knotted.

To be like and equal in all respects to standard sample. No "butts" or pieces in any of the cloths, and no brands on the outside.

Adopted August 30, 1888, *in lieu of specifications of February* 15, 1879, *which are hereby canceled.*

B. C. CARD,

Deputy Quartermaster General, U. S. A., in charge.

2278—F., 1888.

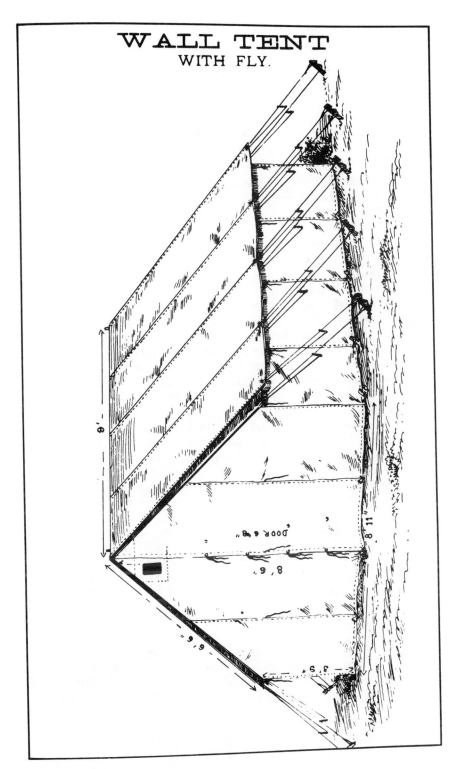

WALL TENT
WITH FLY.

Specifications for Improved Common Tents with Wall (laced corners).

Dimensions.—Dimensions when finished :

Height when pitched	6	feet	10 inches.
Length of ridge	6	"	11 "
Width	8	"	4 "
Height of wall	2	"	0 "
Width of eave	0	"	2 "
Height of door	5	"	6 "
Width of door at top	0	"	3 "
Width of door at bottom	1	"	0 "

Material and Workmanship.—To be made of standard cotton duck twenty-eight and one-half (28½) inches in width, clear of all imperfections, and weighing ten (10) ounces to the linear yard, and in a workmanlike manner, with not less than two and one-half (2½) stitches of equal length to the inch, made with a double thread of five-fold cotton twine well waxed. The seams to be not less than one (1) inch in width, and no slack taken in them.

Door and Stay Pieces.—To be of the same material as the body of the tent. Stay pieces on the ridge to be six and one-half (6½) inches square; those on the corners of the eaves to be sixteen (16) inches long and six (6) inches wide, to be divided eight (8) inches up and eight (8) inches down on the wall; three (3) pieces two (2) inches square to be placed on the side of the end to strengthen door-line holes. Stay pieces triangular in shape stitched across each end next to the ridge, extending five (5) inches below the ridge.

Grommets.—Made with galvanized malleable-iron rings, to be worked in all the holes, and be well made with four-thread five-fold cotton twine well waxed. Eight (8) grommets on the eaves, four (4) on each side of the tent, worked on the seams, size one-half (½) inch; fifteen (15) three-quarter (¾) inch, worked on the foot of the tent; one (1) three-quarter (¾) inch, worked on each end of ridge one and three-eighth (1⅜) inches from the end to the center, of hole; three (3) five-eighth (⅝) inch, worked on the seam of the door at an equal distance of sixteen (16) inches from the foot of the tent; three (3) five-eighth (⅝) inch on the opposite side at the same distance, and one (1) one-half (½) inch, worked at the bottom corner of the door.

Brass Grommets.—Six (6) in number, to be placed on both sides of the door at an equal distance of sixteen (16) inches from the bottom. To be of sheet-brass No. 3.

Sod Cloth.—To be eight and three quarter (8¾) inches wide clear from the tabling, and to extend around the tent from door to door. To be made of standard eight (8) ounce cotton duck.

Foot-stops.—Fifteen (15) in number, to be made in the form of a loop four (4) inches long in the clear of nine (9) thread manila line, both ends passing through a single hole worked in the tabling at the seams and held by the "Mathew Walker" knot. Tabling on the foot to be two (2) inches wide when finished; on the side of the door one and one-half (1½) inches wide.

Door Lines.—To be three (3) feet long, made of six (6) thread manila line (large).

Door Fastenings.—To consist of three (3) double strings of one-quarter (¼) inch cotton rope one (1) foot long in the clear, passing through the grommets worked on the seam, and three (3) on the side of the end for the purpose of tying the door inside; to be secured by a "Mathew Walker" knot.

Eave Lines.—Eight (8) in number, made of six (6) thread manila line (large), to be five (5) feet long in the clear, with an eye spliced on one end four (4) inches long, the other properly whipped and furnished with a metallic slip No. 3.

Wall Lines.—For tying up the wall, to be made of No. 3 gilling line, nineteen (19) in number, to be twenty-four (24) inches long, properly whipped on both ends; four (4) to be placed on each side of the tent in the seams of the wall under the eave, to be sewed on the seams, twenty-three (23) inches above the foot of the tent, passing through with a knot on the inside and stay stitched on the outside; four (4) to be placed on the front end, three (3) on the back end, and one (1) at each corner, as shown in the standard sample.

Laced Corners.—The tabling on the end and side at each corner to be one and one-half (1½) inches wide; five (5) three-eighth (⅜) inch holes to be worked on each corner, over galvanized-iron rings, five (5) inches apart, the lower one taking distance from the center of the grommet hole on the foot of the tent; the opposite side to have five (5) sheet-brass grommets No. 3 placed at the same distance apart, so that the corners may be laced up by means of loops made of No. 3 gilling line, five and one-quarter (5¼) inches long, with the "Mathew Walker" knot on one end; one (1) three-quarter (¾) inch grommet hole worked on each corner for foot-stops.

Ventilator.—An aperture three (3) inches wide and six (6) inches long, one (1) in the front and one (1) in the back end of the tent, placed six (6) inches from the top and two (2) inches from the center, on the right side of each end. The aperture to be reinforced with eight (8) ounce duck.

A flap or curtain on the inside six (6) inches wide and ten (10) inches long, to be made of two-ply eight (8) ounce cotton duck stitched around the edge, with one (1) No. 2 sheet-brass grommet placed at the top for the purpose of tying it up to close the opening; strings made of No. 3 gilling line to be used for tying the curtain in place.

To be like and equal in all respects to the standard sample. No "butts" or pieces in any of the cloths, and no brands on the outside.

Adopted August 30, 1888, *in lieu of specifications of February* 8, 1884, *which are hereby canceled.*

B. C. CARD,

Deputy Quartermaster General, U. S. A., in charge.

2278—F., 1888.

24 tent-pins 16-inch are required for this tent.

COMMON TENT
IMPROVED, LACED CORNERS.

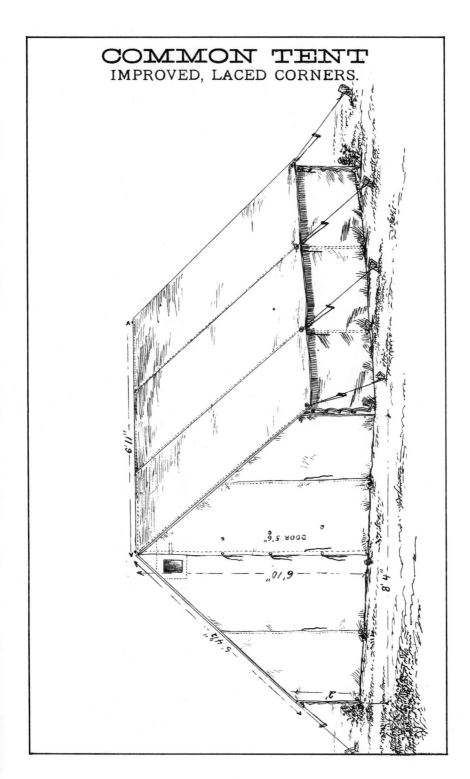

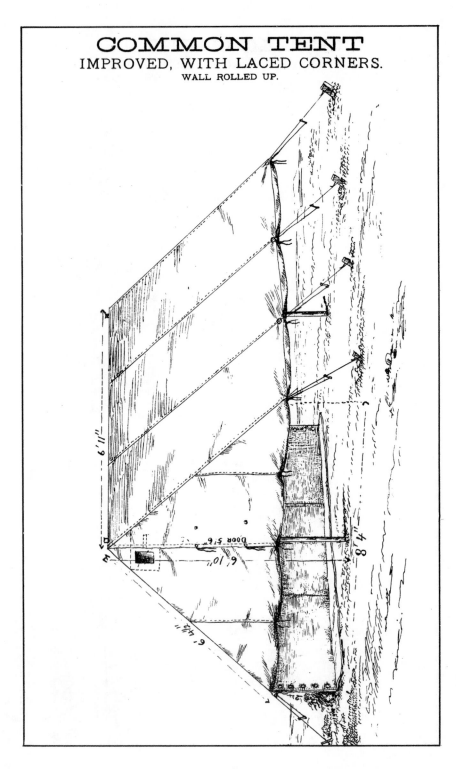

COMMON TENT
IMPROVED, WITH LACED CORNERS.
WALL ROLLED UP.

WAR DEPARTMENT,
QUARTERMASTER GENERAL'S OFFICE.

Specifications for Improved Common Tents with Wall (closed corners).

Dimensions.—Dimensions when finished—

Height when pitched	6 feet 10 inches.
Length of ridge	6 " 11 "
Width	8 " 4 "
Height of wall	2 " 0 "
Width of eave	0 " 2 "
Height of door	5 " 6 "
Width of door at top	0 " 3 "
Width of door at bottom	1 " 0 "

Material and Workmanship.—To be made of standard cotton duck twenty-eight and one-half (28½) inches in width, clear of all imperfections, and weighing ten (10) ounces to the linear yard; and in workmanlike manner, with not less than two and one-half (2½) stitches of equal length to the inch, made with a double thread of five-fold cotton twine well waxed. The seams to be not less than one (1) inch in width, and no slack taken in them.

Door and Stay Pieces.—To be of the same material as the body of the tent. Stay pieces on the ridge to be six and one-half (6½) inches square; those on the corners of the eaves to be sixteen (16) inches long and six (6) inches wide; to be divided eight (8) inches up and eight (8) inches down on the wall; three (3) pieces two (2) inches square to be placed on the side of the end to strengthen door-line holes. Stay pieces triangular in shape, stitched across each end next to the ridge, extending five (5) inches below the ridge.

Grommets.—Made with galvanized malleable-iron rings, to be worked in all the holes, and be well made with four-thread five (5) fold cotton twine well waxed; eight (8) grommets on the eaves, four (4) on each side of the tent, worked on the seams, size, one-half (½) inch; fifteen (15) three-quarter (¾) inch, worked on the foot of the tent; one (1) three-quarter (¾) inch, worked on each end of ridge one and three-eighth (1⅜) inches from the end to the center of hole; three (3) five-eighth (⅝) inch, worked on the seam of the door at an equal distance of sixteen (16) inches from the foot of the tent; three (3) five-eighth (⅝) inch on the opposite side at the same distance, and one (1) one-half (½) inch, worked at the bottom corner of the door.

Brass Grommets.—Six (6) in number, to be placed on both sides of the door at an equal distance of sixteen (16) inches from the bottom. To be of sheet-brass No. 3.

Sod Cloth.—To be eight and three-quarter (8¾) inches wide clear from the tabling, and to extend around the tent from door to door. To be made of standard eight (8) ounce cotton duck.

Foot-stops.—Fifteen (15) in number, to be made in the form of a loop four (4) inches long in the clear, of nine (9) thread manila line, both ends passing through a single hole worked in the tabling at the seams and held by the "Mathew Walker" knot. Tabling on the foot to be two (2) inches wide when finished; on the side of the door one and one-half (1½) inches wide.

Door Lines.—To be three (3) feet long, made of six (6) thread manila line (large).

Door Fastenings.—To consist of three (3) double strings of one-quarter (¼) inch cotton rope one (1) foot long in the clear, passing through the grommets worked on the seam, and three (3) on the side of the end, for the purpose of tying the door inside; to be secured by a "Mathew Walker" knot.

Eave Lines.—Eight (8) in number, made of six (6) thread manila line (large), to be five (5) feet long in the clear, with an eye spliced on one end four (4) inches long; the other properly whipped, and furnished with a metallic slip No. 3.

Wall Lines.—For tying up the wall, to be made of No. 3 gilling line, fifteen (15) in number, to be twenty-four (24) inches long, properly whipped on both ends; four (4) to be placed on each side of the tent in the seams of the wall under the eave, to be sewed on the seams twenty-three (23) inches above the foot of the tent, passing through with a knot on the inside and stay stitched on the outside; four (4) to be placed on the front end, three (3) on the back end, and one (1) at each corner, as shown in the standard sample.

Ventilator.—An aperture three (3) inches wide and six (6) inches long, one (1) in the front and one (1) in the back end of the tent, placed six (6) inches from the top and two (2) inches from the center, on the right side of each end. The aperture to be reinforced with eight (8) ounce duck. A flap or curtain on the inside, six (6) inches wide and ten (10) inches long, to be made of two-ply eight (8) ounce duck stitched around the edge, with one (1) No. 2 sheet-brass grommet placed at the top for the purpose of tying it up to close the opening; strings made of No. 3 gilling line to be used for tying the curtain in place. To be like and equal in all respects to the standard sample. No "butts" or pieces in any of the cloths, and no brands on the outside.

Adopted August 30, 1888, in lieu of specifications of February 8, 1884, which are hereby canceled.

B. C. CARD,

Deputy Quartermaster General, U. S. A., in charge.

2278—F., 1888.

24 tent-pins 16-inch are required for this tent.

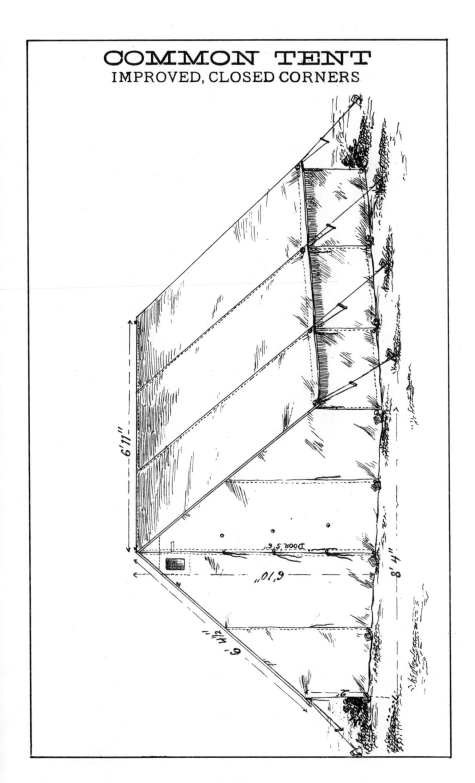

COMMON TENT
IMPROVED, CLOSED CORNERS

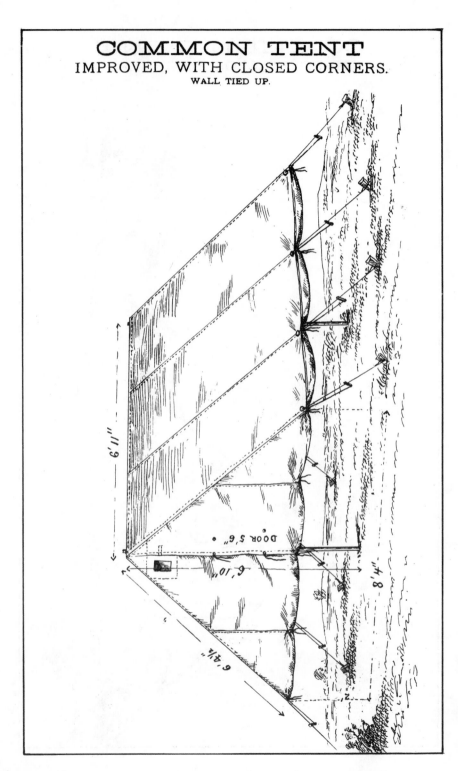

COMMON TENT
IMPROVED, WITH CLOSED CORNERS.
WALL TIED UP.

DOOR 5'6"

6' 11"

6' 10"

8' 4"

6' 4½"

WAR DEPARTMENT,

QUARTERMASTER GENERAL'S OFFICE.

Specifications for Corn Brooms.

The body of the broom is to be made of the best broom corn, strong and pliable, about sixteen (16) inches long from neck to end, with fine hurl on outside.

To be held in shape by three ties of strong, well-waxed twine, five-eighths (5/8) of an inch apart, the lower tie to be about five (5) inches distant from neck. At the middle the broom must be perfectly solid, about seven (7) inches wide and (1) one inch thick, spreading at the end to a width of about thirteen (13) inches.

The upper end of the broom is to be fastened around the handle by eight (8) strands of No. 19 (American gauge) annealed wire, tinned, nearest to the body of the broom, three (3) strands near the handle, and three (3) strands between these two fastenings.

The handle, made of basswood, is to be about thirty-eight (38) inches long in the clear, and one and one-eighth (1 1/8) inches diameter at lower end, and seven-eighths (7/8) inch diameter at top.

The brooms to be of uniform weight, not less than twenty-one (21) pounds to the dozen.

The broom accepted as Army standard is in the trade known as "three-string hurl broom."

Adopted December 3, 1888, in lieu of specifications of May 31, 1876, which are hereby canceled.

S. B. HOLABIRD,
Quartermaster General, U. S. A.

3199—F., 1888.

BROOM.

WAR DEPARTMENT,
QUARTERMASTER GENERAL'S OFFICE.

Specifications for Forage Caps.

Cloth.—To be made of wool-dyed indigo-blue cloth, fifty-four (54) inches in width, and to weigh not less than thirteen (13) ounces to the linear yard; to contain forty-eight (48) threads to the inch in the warp and forty-six (46) threads to the inch in the filling; to be capable of sustaining a strain of twenty-six (26) pounds to the inch in the warp and eighteen (18) pounds to the inch in the filling, and to be well sponged before being made up into caps.

Band.—The band to be about one and three-eighths (1⅜) inches wide, strengthened by a strip of strong split leather, of the same width, sewed in between the cloth and the sweat-leather.

Front.—The front to rise above the band straight and vertical one and one-eighth (1⅛) inches, sides slightly converging from the band to the crown.

Back.—The back to be slightly convex, four and one-half (4½) inches long from the band, from which it rises at an angle of forty-five (45) degrees to the crown.

Crown.—The crown to be circular, five (5) inches in diameter, made upon strong "tarred board," covered on the inside with black enameled muslin. The shape of the cap would thus give an incline to the crown of about one (1) inch from the rear to front.

Visor.—To have a straight horizontal visor of patent enameled leather, black above and green underneath, about three-sixteenths (3/16) of an inch thick, bound with fine black enameled leather, and shaped to conform to the standard sample.

Trimmings.—A small regulation button (line or staff, as may be required) on each side, immediately behind the ends of the visor, for chin-strap. The side buttons to be fire-gilt. The chin strap to be made of good enameled leather in two (2) parts, each part about nine (9) inches long and one-half (½) inch wide, and fitted with a stout fire-gilt slide on the end of the under part, and leather keeper on the end of the upper part, through which the end, finished to a point, will project about one-half (½) an inch, to permit the strap to be adjusted at will. Sweat-leather of Belgian leather, one and one-half (1½) inches wide.   Lining of strong black satin, fastened by its lower edge only to the inner stiffening of the band, the upper edge gathered with strong thread over an elastic cord.   Each cap to be furnished with a loop of black mohair or worsted braid one-eighth ($\frac{1}{8}$) of an inch wide, and securely fastened under the sweat-leather at the back seam.

Materials, workmanship, and finish to conform to standard sample.

Adopted January 5, 1889, in lieu of specifications of April 15, 1886, which are hereby canceled.

S. B. HOLABIRD,
Quartermaster General, U. S. A.

54—F., 1889.

FORAGE CAP.

Specifications for Tent-Pins.

Material.—Of white or red oak, or of hickory, osage orange, or Bois d'Arc, straight-grained and free from knots or other imperfections. Pins to be split, not sawed.

Dimensions.—*For Hospital Tents :* The large pins to be twenty-six (26) inches long, one and five-eighths (1⅝) inches wide, and one (1) inch thick : the first notch four (4) inches from top and the second notch ten (10) inches from top. The small pins to be twenty (20) inches long, one and five-eighths (1⅝) inches wide, and one (1) inch thick, and to have one (1) notch three (3) inches from top.

For Wall Tents.—The large pins to be twenty-four (24) inches long, one and one-half (1½) inches wide, and one (1) inch thick ; the first notch to be three and one-half (3½) inches from top and the second notch eight (8) inches from top. The small pins to be sixteen (16) inches long, one and three-eighths (1⅜) inches wide, and one (1) inch thick, one (1) notch three (3) inches from top.

For Common Tents.—To be sixteen (16) inches long, one and three-eighths (1⅜) inches wide, and one (1) inch thick, one (1) notch three (3) inches from top.

For Shelter Tents.—To be nine (9) inches long and about one (1) inch in diameter ; head in form of frustum of cone, about seven-eighths (⅞) of an inch high, and neck turned down to a diameter of about five-eighths (⅝) of an inch. Largest diameter about three and one-half (3½) inches from top, and gradually turned down to a point at bottom.

Each conical-wall tent requires forty-eight (48) small pins. Each hospital tent requires eighteen (18) large and twenty-eight (28) small pins. Each wall tent requires ten (10) large and eighteen (18) small pins. Each common tent requires twenty-four (24) pins. Each shelter tent requires eight (8) pins.

Adopted January 5, 1889, in lieu of specifications of October 1, 1879, which are hereby canceled.

S. B. HOLABIRD,

Quartermaster General, U. S. A.

54—F., 1889.

TENT PINS.

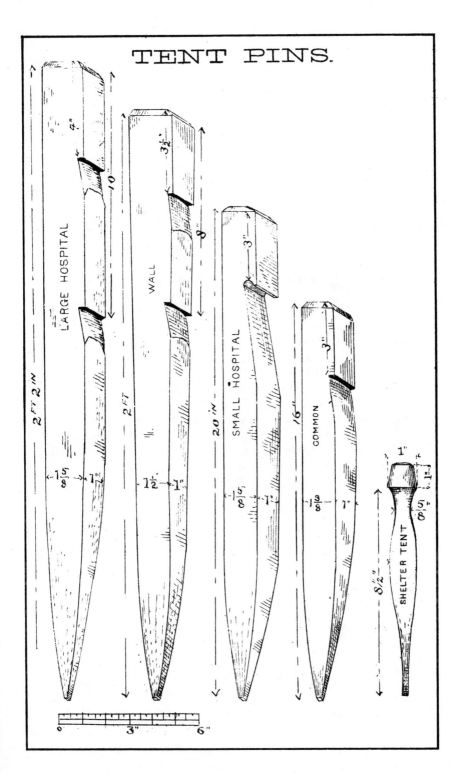

WAR DEPARTMENT,

QUARTERMASTER GENERAL'S OFFICE.

Specifications for Conical Wall-Tent Poles.

Material.—To be made of first quality white pine or ash, straight-grained.

Size.—To be seven (7) feet nine (9) inches long, two and three-fourths (2¾) inches in diameter, tapered to two and one-half (2½) inches at the top, and to two (2) inches at the bottom.

To have a galvanized-iron band at the top two and one-half (2½) inches deep, one-eighth (⅛) inch thick, put on flush with the pole, and secured by two (2) three-quarter (¾) inch screws.

To have a galvanized-iron spindle one-half (½) inch thick, projecting three (3) inches from the top, and extending into the pole three (3) inches.

To be equal in quality and finish to the standard samples.

Adopted January 5, 1889.

S. B. HOLABIRD,
Quartermaster General, U. S. A.

54—F., 1889.

WAR DEPARTMENT,

QUARTERMASTER GENERAL'S OFFICE.

Specifications for Metal Tent-Slips.

To be made of red brass (consisting of copper and tin) in three sizes. No. 1 to be five (5) inches long, No. 2 to be four (4) inches long, and No. 3 to be three (3) inches long.

To be semi-tubular in form, except at one end, which is covered or tubular to the depth on—

No. 1, of three-fourths ($\frac{3}{4}$) of an inch; No. 2, of five-eighths ($\frac{5}{8}$) of an inch; and No. 3, of one-half ($\frac{1}{2}$) of an an inch.

The semi-tubular end to have a hole sufficiently large to receive the various sizes of tent line upon which they are used, *i. e.*, three-fourths ($\frac{3}{4}$) of an inch in diameter, eleven-sixteenths ($\frac{11}{16}$) of an inch in diameter, and nine-sixteenths ($\frac{9}{16}$) of an inch in diameter.

To weigh as follows:

No. 1, six (6) to the pound; No. 2, eight (8) to the pound, and No. 3, fifteen (15) to the pound.

All holes to be finished by removing the sharp edges.

To be like in form, quality, finish, and weight to the standard samples.

Adopted January 5, 1889.

S. B. HOLABIRD,
Quartermaster General, U. S. A.

54—F., 1889.

METAL TENT SLIPS.

N° 1

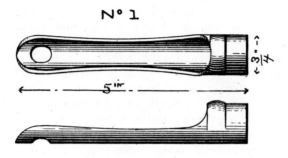

5 ᵢₙ. $\frac{3}{4}$"

N° 2

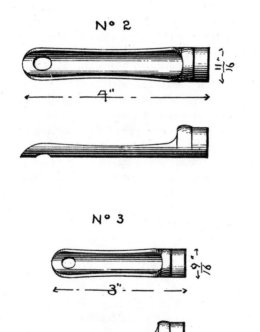

4" $\frac{11}{16}$"

N° 3

3" $\frac{9}{16}$"

WAR DEPARTMENT,
QUARTERMASTER GENERAL'S OFFICE.

Specifications for Hand Litters.

Side and end rails to be made of straight-grained ash, free from knots or other imperfections. Side rails to be eight (8) feet nine (9) inches long and one and one-half (1½) inches in diameter. End rails to be the same thickness as the side rails, two (2) feet long between side rails, to which they are to fit by being hollowed out in the ends.

Each side rail to have two (2) iron rings five-eighth (⅝) inch wide, one-eighth (⅛) inch thick, securely riveted thereto sixteen (16) inches from each end, as stops for the end rails.

Attached to each end rail will be supports, standing twelve (12) inches above the ground, made of band iron one (1) inch wide and one-quarter (¼) inch thick, fashioned and bent to form legs, and also sockets through which the side rails are to pass in putting the parts together, as per sample. In each end rail there are to be three (3) three-eighth (⅜) inch bolts passing through the rail and riveted over a washer, the head of the bolts to project three-quarters (¾) of an inch above the rail, forming pins upon which to adjust and tighten the canvas bottom of the litter.

To have a canvas bottom five (5) feet eight (8) inches long, made of No. 4 canvas twenty-two (22) inches wide, two widths sewed together, making a seam one and one-half (1½) inches wide down the center; the outer edges turned over seven (7) inches and securely sewed, forming loops the whole length of the bottom for the side rails to pass through. Seams at top and bottom to be two (2) inches wide. At the top, three (3) turned grommets, two (2) inches long, made of tarred ratlin-line, securely sewed in proper places to hook on the pins in the top end rail. At the bottom, three (3) turned grommets, worked on the seams in proper places for the tightening line.

Tightening line to be made of nine-thread manila rope, spliced in the left-hand grommet, three (3) feet six (6) inches long, finished; whipped on loose end.

Each litter to be furnished with two (2) carrying straps, made of first-class bridle-leather, six (6) feet two (2) inches long and two (2) inches wide, made with a loop four (4) inches long on one end, the other end made with a roller buckle of japanned iron; rigged to form an adjustable loop.

Workmanship and finish of whole to conform to standard sample.

Adopted January 5, 1889.

S. B. HOLABIRD,
Quartermaster General, U. S. A.

54—F., 1889.

236

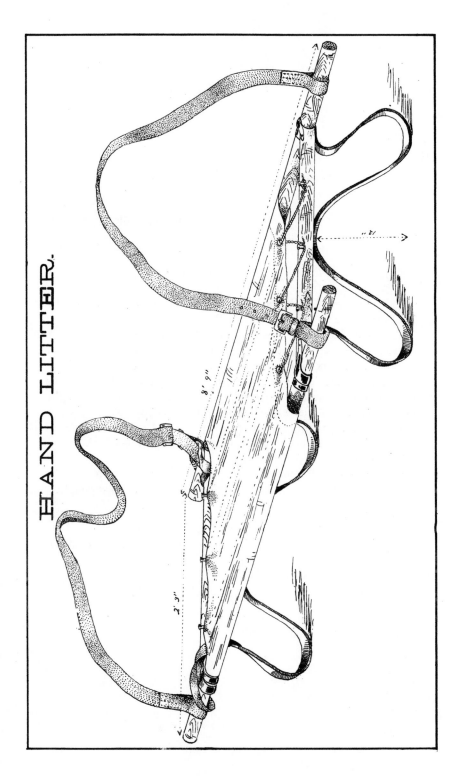

HAND LITTER.

WAR DEPARTMENT,

QUARTERMASTER GENERAL'S OFFICE.

Specifications for Rubber Blankets.

To be forty-five (45) by seventy-two (72) inches of sixteen (16) by sixteen (16) sheeting, coated with rubber, luster finish.

To have eighteen (18) brass grommets (one-quarter ($\frac{1}{4}$) inch inside diameter) inserted along the edges, and arranged so as to show four (4) on each end, six (6) on one side, and eight (8) on the other side, as per standard sample. The grommets on one side and end to be inserted two (2) inches from center to edge of blanket, and on the other side and end one (1) inch from center to edge of blanket, which is to have a flat rubber ribbon binding one-half ($\frac{1}{2}$) inch wide all around. Each grommet to be reinforced with the rubber fabric one and one-half ($1\frac{1}{2}$) inches square.

Average weight of blanket to be two and one-half ($2\frac{1}{2}$) pounds.

Material, workmanship, and finish to conform to standard sample.

Adopted January 5, 1889.

S. B. HOLABIRD,
Quartermaster General, U. S. A.

54—F., 1889.

RUBBER BLANKET.

6'

3' 9"

WAR DEPARTMENT,
QUARTERMASTER GENERAL'S OFFICE.

Specifications for Rubber Ponchos.

To be forty-five (45) by seventy-two (72) inches of sixteen (16) by sixteen (16) sheeting, coated with rubber, luster finish.

To have an opening fourteen (14) inches long, crosswise in the center, covered by a flap of same fabric as above described, two and one-half (2½) inches wide, and finished with a button and button-hole in the center of the opening.

To have sixteen (16) brass grommets (one-quarter (¼) inch inside diameter) inserted along the edges so as to show four (4) at ends and six (6) at sides, as per standard sample. On one side and end the grommets to be inserted two (2) inches from center to edge of poncho, and on the other side and end one (1) inch from center to edge of poncho, which is to have a flat rubber ribbon binding one-half (½) inch wide all around. Each grommet to be reinforced with the rubber fabric one and one-half (1½) inches square.

Average weight of poncho to be two and one-half (2½) pounds.

Material, workmanship, and finish to conform to standard sample.

Adopted January 5, 1889.

S. B. HOLABIRD,
Quartermaster General, U. S. A.

54—F., 1889.

RUBBER PONCHO.

WAR DEPARTMENT,

QUARTERMASTER GENERAL'S OFFICE.

Specifications for Camp Colors.

Material.—To be of one piece of bunting of best quality.

Design.—Same as for garrison flag, and to be produced by clamp dyeing the blue field and red stripes on white bunting.

Size.—To be twenty (20) inches fly, exclusive of pike-casing, and eighteen (18) inches on the pike. The pike-casing to be formed by turning over the end next to the field of sufficient width to admit the pike.

Pike.—To be of straight-grained and seasoned ash, fitted with an adjustable cone at the head and a pointed brass ferrule at the foot. Total length about eight (8) feet.

Workmanship and finish.—To conform to standard sample.

Adopted January 5, 1889.

S. B. HOLABIRD,
Quartermaster General, U. S. A.

54—F., 1889.

CAMP COLOR.

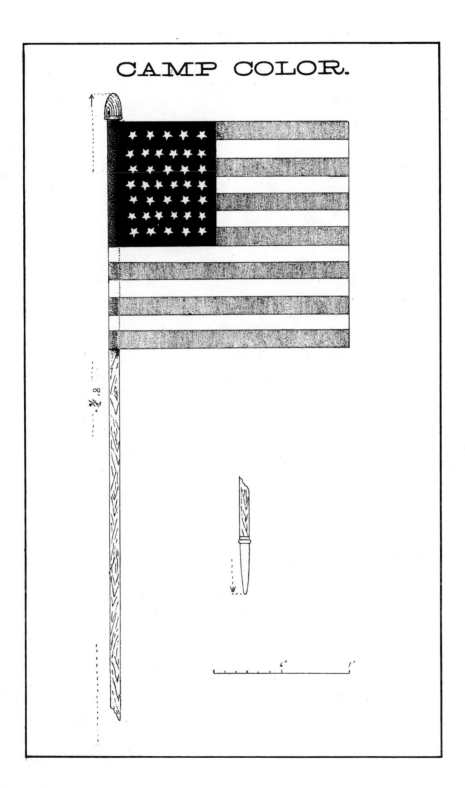

WAR DEPARTMENT,

QUARTERMASTER GENERAL'S OFFICE,

Specifications for Drum-Sticks.

To be made of ebony wood, lightly polished; to be seventeen (17) inches long, thirteen-sixteenths ($\frac{13}{16}$) of an inch in diameter at the butt end, and round on the top, tapered to six-sixteenths ($\frac{6}{16}$) of an inch to within one and one-half (1½) inches of the outer end, which is to be finished with an oval pear-shaped point five-eighths (⅝) of an inch in diameter at the center.

To be equal in quality, form, and finish to the standard sample.

Adopted January 5, 1889.

S. B. HOLABIRD,
Quartermaster General, U. S. A.

54—F.. 1889.

DRUM STICKS.

WAR DEPARTMENT,
Quartermaster General's Office.

Specifications for Axes.

To be made of the best extra refined iron with best cast-steel blades and polls, lap-welded. To be of the standard pattern, and perfect in the welds and eyes.

To be furnished in the following weights: three and one-half (3½) pounds, three and three-quarters (3¾) pounds, and four (4) pounds, as required.

Adopted January 5, 1889.

S. B. HOLABIRD,
Quartermaster General, U. S. A.

54—F., 1889.

AXE.

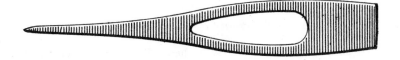

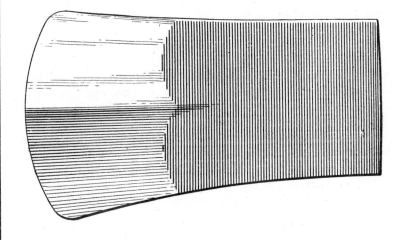

WAR DEPARTMENT,

QUARTERMASTER GENERAL'S OFFICE.

Specifications for Ax-Slings.

To be made of black harness leather. The body or pocket of the sling to be of one piece of leather cut to the form of the standard sample, twenty (20) inches long and six (6) inches deep, folded and substantially sewed together at the blade end, with a strip three-quarters (¾) of an inch wide of the same kind of leather inserted. The bottom to be spread at the pole end by the insertion in the seam of six (6) layers of leather one-half (½) inch wide, shaved down and reduced to two (2) layers as they approach the blade end, giving the sling the form of an ax head, and forming a pocket for the same. This sling or pocket to have a strap one (1) inch wide and fifty-eight (58) inches long, made in two parts, one part seventeen (17) inches long, finished with a roller buckle and keeper, and leather shield behind the buckle; the other part to be forty-one (41) inches long, and supplied with a leather loop about two and one-half (2½) inches in diameter for the handle of the ax, and to have a leather strap one-half (½) inch wide and eight (8) inches long, securely sewed to the back side, and a corresponding buckle for the same on the front side to secure the ax in the sling.

All sewing to be done with good and strong waxed linen thread and in the best workmanlike manner.

Materials and workmanship to conform to standard sample.

Adopted January 5, 1889.

S. B. HOLABIRD,
Quartermaster General, U. S. A.

54—F., 1889.

AXE SLING.

WAR DEPARTMENT,

QUARTERMASTER GENERAL'S OFFICE.

Specifications for Pick-Axes.

To be made of the best extra refined iron with best cast-steel points and blades, properly welded in all parts. The eyes to be regular and uniform in size to fit standard handles.

To weigh seven (7) pounds each and be like and equal to the standard sample.

Adopted January 5, 1889.

S. B. HOLABIRD,
Quartermaster General, U. S. A.

54—F., 1889.

WAR DEPARTMENT,

QUARTERMASTER GENERAL'S OFFICE.

Specifications for Pick-Ax Helves.

Material.—To be of good seasoned, straight-grained hickory, free from knots and shakes, and to be polished.

Size.—To be thirty-six (36) inches long and fashioned on the end to fit the eye of the "Pick-Ax."

Workmanship and finish.—To be equal in quality, shape, and finish to the standard sample.

Adopted January 5, 1889.

S. B. HOLABIRD,
Quartermaster General, U. S. A.

54—F., 1889.

PICK-AXE & HANDLE.

WAR DEPARTMENT,

QUARTERMASTER GENERAL'S OFFICE.

Specifications for Camp Hatchets (ax-shaped).

To be made of the best refined cast-steel; the blade to be tipped with the best forged steel one (1) inch deep.

To be of standard pattern and perfect in the welds and eyes.

To weigh one and one-fourth (1¼) pounds.

Adopted January 5, 1889.

S. B. HOLABIRD,
Quartermaster General, U. S. A.

54—F., 1889.

WAR DEPARTMENT,

QUARTERMASTER GENERAL'S OFFICE

Specifications for Hatchet Helves.

To be made of good seasoned straight-grained hickory, free from knots or shakes. To be thirteen (13) inches long, oval in form, one and one-half (1½) inches by one (1) inch at the swell of the handle.

To be properly formed and polished, and to have a saw cut in the upper end one and one-half (1½) to two (2) inches deep to receive a wedge, and fashioned to the form of the eye of a hatchet.

To be equal in quality and finish to the standard sample.

Adopted January 5, 1889.

S. B. HOLABIRD,
Quartermaster General, U. S. A.

54—F., 1889.

HATCHET
WITH HANDLE.

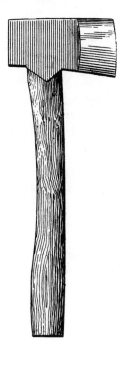

QUARTERMASTER GENERAL'S OFFICE.

Specifications for Spades.

Material.—To be made of the best cast-steel.

Size.—The blade to be of No. 8 gauge, twelve (12) inches deep, seven and one-quarter (7¼) inches broad at the top, tapered to six and seven-eighths (6⅞) inches at the bottom. The straps for the handle connected with the plates forming the blade and extending nine and five-eighths (9⅝) inches on the handle, and secured thereto with three (3) rivets, two (2) above the blade and one (1) one and one-half (1½) inches below the top of the blade. The top of the blade on each side of the handle to be covered with iron plates, mortised on.

Handle.—The handle to be of white oak or good straight-grained and seasoned ash, free from knots or other imperfections, one and one-half (1½) inches diameter, two (2) feet two (2) inches long, properly formed ; making the length of the spade three (3) feet two and one-half (2½) inches.

To be equal in quality, size, and finish to the standard sample.

Adopted January 5, 1889.

S. B. HOLABIRD,
Quartermaster General, U. S. A.

54—F., 1889.

SPADE.

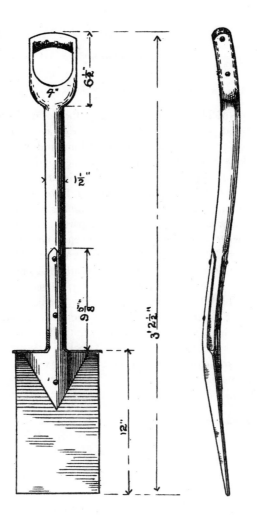

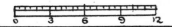

Specifications for Spade Slings.

To be made of black harness leather in the form of the blade of a spade, eight and one-quarter (8¼) inches wide at the top, seven and three-quarters (7¾) inches wide at the bottom, and eleven (11) inches deep. To have strips of leather at least one-quarter (¼) of an inch thick and one-half (½) of an inch wide, inserted in the side and bottom seams to form a pocket. To be furnished with a leather carrying strap one and one-quarter (1¼) inches wide and sixty-three (63) inches long, made in two parts; one part fifteen (15) inches long, and finished with a roller buckle, leather keeper, and shield; the other part to be forty-eight (48) inches long, and finished with a leather strap and buckle ten (10) inches long, five-eighths (⅝) of an inch wide, placed eighteen (18) inches from the pocket, to secure the handle of the spade; to have two (2) straps, each nine (9) inches long and three-quarters (¾) of an inch wide, sewed to the back of the pocket, and corresponding buckles properly placed on the front of the same for the purpose of securing the spade in the pocket.

All sewing to be done with the best linen waxed thread, and in a workmanlike manner.

Materials and workmanship to conform to standard sample.

Adopted January 5, 1889.

S. B. HOLABIRD,
Quartermaster General, U. S. A.

54—F., 1889.

SPADE SLING.

Specifications for Shovels, long handles.

Material and size.—To be made of the best cast-steel, No. 13 gauge; the blade to be twelve (12) inches deep, nine and one-half (9½) inches wide at the top, and symmetrically rounded to a point at the edge; with back strap and stays extending eleven (11) inches on the handle, and **V**-shaped, five (5) inches by five (5) inches on the back, well secured by five (5) rivets on the back and three (3) rivets through the handle, the front strap ending in a **V**-shaped plate two (2) inches by two and one-half (2½) inches on the plate of the shovel, and secured by three (3) rivets.

Handle—To be of the best straight-grained ash, free from knots and shakes, properly formed; one and one-half (1½) inches in diameter, and four (4) feet two and one-quarter (2¼) inches above the blade, making the extreme length of the shovel five (5) feet two and one-quarter (2¼) inches.

Workmanship and finish.—To conform to the standard sample.

Adopted January 5, 1889.

S. B. HOLABIRD,
Quartermaster General, U. S. A.

54—F., 1889.

SHOVEL.

LONG HANDLE.

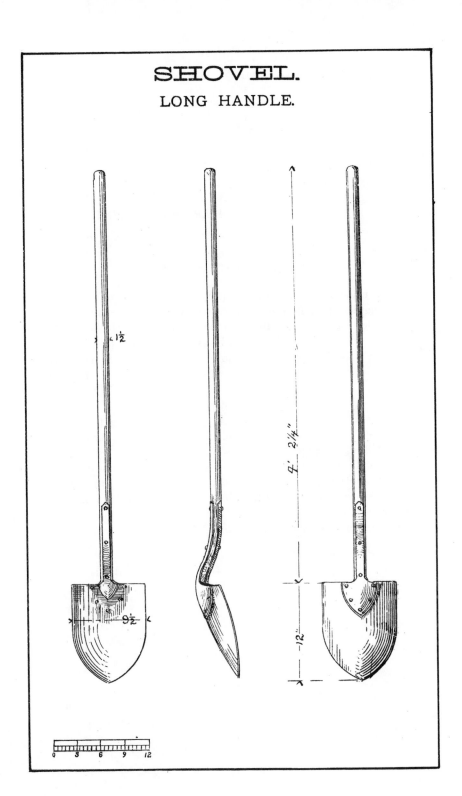

WAR DEPARTMENT,

Quartermaster General's Office.

Specifications for Shovels, Short Handles.

To be made of the best cast-steel, No. 13 gauge, properly formed, and strengthened by front and back straps and stays extending up on the handle nine and one-half (9½) inches, the stay attached to the front strap **V**-shaped, two (2) inches by two and one-half (2½) inches, extending upon the plate of the shovel, secured by three (3) rivets. The **V**-shaped stay, five (5) inches by five (5) inches, attached to the back strap, secured by five (5) rivets through the plate of the shovel, and three (3) rivets through the handle.

The blade or plate to be twelve (12) inches deep, eight and five-eighths (8⅝) inches broad at the top, and nine and three-fourths (9¾) inches wide at the edge.

The handle to be made of the best straight-grained, seasoned ash, free from knots and shakes, properly formed and secured to the shovel, making the extreme length of the same three (3) feet one and one-half (1½) inches.

To conform to the standard sample.

Adopted January 5, 1889.

S. B. HOLABIRD,
Quartermaster General, U. S. A.

54—F., 1889.

SHOVELS.

SHORT HANDLE.

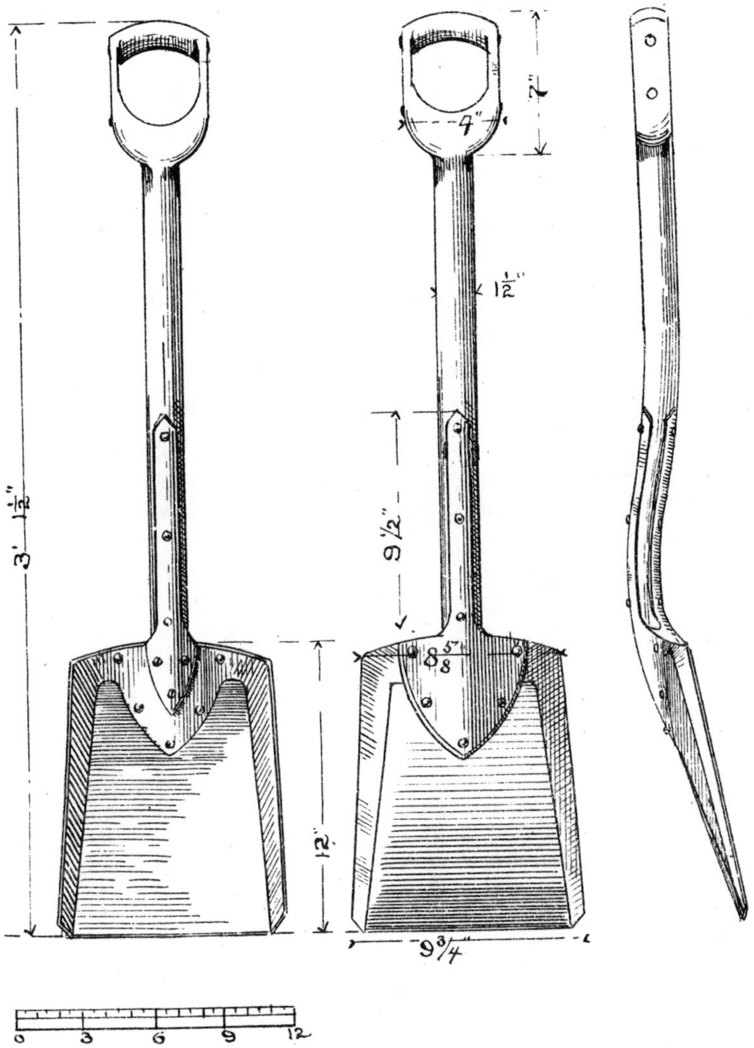

3' 1½"

7"

4"

1½"

9½"

8⅝"

12"

9¾"

0   3   6   9   12

WAR DEPARTMENT,

QUARTERMASTER GENERAL'S OFFICE.

Specifications for Mess-Pans.

Material.—To be made of No. 24 "bloom iron," the upper edge turned over No. 9 iron wire.

Dimensions.—To be eleven and three-quarters (11¾) inches in diameter at the top, eight and one-quarter (8¼) inches at the bottom, and five and one-quarter (5¼) inches deep.

Workmanship and finish.—The seams on each side and bottom to be lapped and closely and neatly set, and equal in quality and finish to the standard sample.

Weight.—To weigh two (2) pounds.

Adopted January 5, 1889.

S. B. HOLABIRD,
Quartermaster General, U. S. A.

54—F., 1889.

MESS PAN.

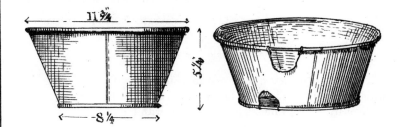

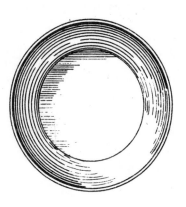

WAR DEPARTMENT,

Quartermaster General's Office.

Specifications for Iron Pots.

To be made of best quality cast-iron, bulge shaped and flaring top, with lugs cast on the sides for handle, and three (3) legs three and three-quarters (3¾) inches long, also cast with the pot.

Capacity.—Six (6) gallons.

To have handle made of three-eighths (⅜) inch round iron, measuring thirty (30) inches from lug to lug when properly fitted to the pot.

To weigh about thirty-six (36) pounds.

To be like in form and equal in quality and size to the standard sample.

Adopted January 5, 1889.

S. B. HOLABIRD,
Quartermaster General, U. S. A.

54—F., 1889.

IRON POT.

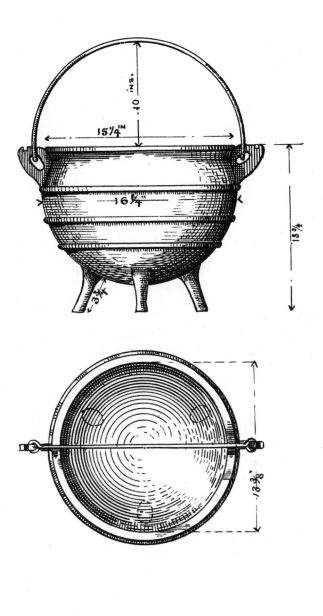

WAR DEPARTMENT,

QUARTERMASTER GENERAL'S OFFICE.

Specifications for Camp Kettles.

Material.—To be made of No. 24 "bloom iron," the upper edge turned over No. 7 iron wire, the handles to be one-quarter ($\frac{1}{4}$) inch round iron.

Sizes.—To be in nests of three sizes: large, medium, and small. The large size to be twelve (12) inches in diameter and eleven and one-quarter ($11\frac{1}{4}$) inches deep. The medium size to be ten and one-quarter ($10\frac{1}{4}$) inches in diameter and eleven (11) inches deep. The small size to be nine (9) inches in diameter and ten and three-quarters ($10\frac{3}{4}$) inches deep.

Workmanship.—Each kettle to have the handle hooked on from the outside, so as to hang about two and one-half ($2\frac{1}{2}$) inches from the top. The seams on the side and around the bottom to be lapped and closely and neatly set.

To be equal in quality, size, and workmanship and finish to the standard sample.

Adopted January 5, 1889.

S. B. HOLABIRD,
Quartermaster General, U. S. A.

54—F., 1889.

CAMP KETTLES.

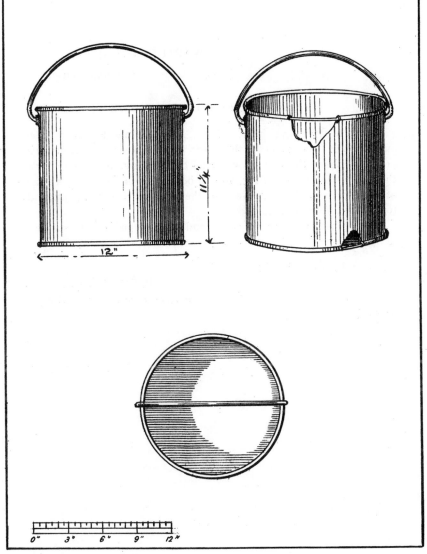

WAR DEPARTMENT,

QUARTERMASTER GENERAL'S OFFICE.

Specifications for Black Italian Cloth.

To be fifty-four (54) inches wide. To weigh not less than seven and one-half (7½) ounces so the linear yard. To contain one hundred (100) threads to the inch of warp and one hundred and twelve (112) threads to the inch of filling, and to be capable of sustaining a strain of fifty (50) pounds to the inch in the warp and twenty (20) pounds to the inch in the filling.

To be, in quality, weave, color, and finish, equal to the standard sample.

Adopted January 5, 1889.

S. B. HOLABIRD,
Quartermaster General, U. S. A.

54—F., 1889.

WAR DEPARTMENT,

QUARTERMASTER GENERAL'S OFFICE.

Specifications for Cotton Drilling (unbleached).

To be full thirty (30) inches wide when finished. To contain not less than sixty-eight (68) threads to the inch of warp and sixty (60) threads to the inch of filling. To weigh not less than six (6) ounces to the linear yard. To be capable of sustaining a strain of ninety (90) pounds to the inch of warp and sixty-seven (67) pounds to the inch of filling.

To be in quality, weave, and finish equal to the standard sample.

Adopted January 5, 1889.

S. B. HOLABIRD,
Quartermaster General, U. S. A.

54—F., 1889.

WAR DEPARTMENT,

QUARTERMASTER GENERAL'S OFFICE.

Specifications for Black Padding.

To be equal in quality, weave, color, and finish to the standard sample.

To be full twenty-seven (27) inches wide. To contain not less than forty-eight (48) threads to the inch of warp and sixty-eight (68) threads to the inch of filling.

To weigh not less than six (6) ounces to the yard.

Adopted January 5, 1889.

S. B. HOLABIRD,
Quartermaster General, U. S. A.

54—F., 1889.

WAR DEPARTMENT,

QUARTERMASTER GENERAL'S OFFICE.

Specifications for Canvas Padding.

To be full twenty-five (25) inches wide. To contain not less than thirty-six (36) threads to the inch in the warp and forty (40) threads to the inch in the filling. To weigh not less than six and one-half (6½) ounces to the linear yard, and be capable of sustaining a strain of ninety (90) pounds to the inch in the warp and eighty-five (85) pounds to the inch in the filling.

To be in quality, weave, and finish equal to the standard sample.

Adopted January 5, 1889.

S. B. HOLABIRD,
Quartermaster General, U. S. A.

54—F., 1889.

WAR DEPARTMENT,

QUARTERMASTER GENERAL'S OFFICE.

Specifications for Unbleached Muslin.

To be thirty-six (36) inches wide, free from imperfections.

To contain seventy-two (72) threads to the inch of warp and seventy-six (76) threads to the inch of filling. To weigh not less than (5) ounces to the linear yard, and be capable of sustaining a strain of sixty (60) pounds to the inch in the warp and fifty (50) pounds to the inch in the filling.

To be equal in quality, weave, and finish to the standard sample.

Adopted February 20, 1889.

S. B. HOLABIRD,
Quartermaster General, U. S. A.

463 – F., 1889.

WAR DEPARTMENT,

QUARTERMASTER GENERAL'S OFFICE.

Specifications for Black Silesia.

To be in quality, weave, color, and finish equal to the standard sample; full thirty-six (36) inches wide; to contain not less than ninety (90) threads to the inch in the warp and seventy-four (74) threads to the inch in the filling. To weigh not less than five (5) ounces to the linear yard, and be capable of sustaining a strain of sixty (60) pounds to the inch of warp and fifty (50) pounds to the inch of filling.

Adopted February 20, 1889.

S. B. HOLABIRD,
Quartermaster General, U. S. A.

463—F., 1889.

WAR DEPARTMENT,

Quartermaster General's Office.

Specifications for Arctic Overshoes.

Fronts and quarters to be made of black tweed waterproof with scarlet fleece lining, held together by an inner coating of India rubber. Vulcanized rubber foxing around the entire shoe, to rise at heel sufficiently to cover counter, to be about one (1) inch deep at sides forward of heel, and to rise at toe to a height of about one and one-half (1½) inches at center. Tap sole and tap heel of vulcanized rubber; bottoms rough; average height about ten (10) inches from heel to top of upper at back. Front and quarter joined by a gore of same material so as to exclude snow, water, etc.

Fastenings at front to consist of two (2) straps and two (2) buckles, with rivet at each buckle and strap. Front and quarters secured by rivet at each side.

Average weight about three (3) pounds and eight (8) ounces per pair. (No. 9 shoe taken as the standard for weight and measurement.)

The overshoes to conform in material, pattern, and workmanship to the standard sample.

Adopted January 18, 1889, in lieu of specifications of May 5, 1876, which are hereby canceled.

S. B. HOLABIRD,
Quartermaster General, U. S. A.

202—F., 1889.

ARCTIC OVER SHOES.

WAR DEPARTMENT,

Quartermaster General's Office.

Specifications for Shelter Tents (Halves).

Material.—To be made of cotton duck, thirty-three and one-half (33½) inches wide, weighing eight (8) ounces to the linear yard, and free from imperfections.

Dimensions and Workmanship.—To be sixty-six (66) inches long at the top and sixty-five (65) inches wide when finished. The center seam to overlap one (1) inch. The four corners and center at the bottom of each half tent to be reinforced with pieces of the same material firmly sewed on, said pieces to be four (4) inches square when finished. The top and bottom edges of each half tent to be turned in and hemmed, making one-quarter (¼) inch seams, neatly and securely sewed. To have two (2) grommet-holes worked at each corner and at center of bottom; those at the upper corners two (2) inches from the top, and the first one one and one-half (1½) inches from the edge, and one and one-half (1½) inches from center to center apart; those at the bottom to be one and one-half (1½) inches from the lower edge and in line with those at the top. To have nine (9) buttons and button-holes along the top; the first button-hole one (1) inch from the edge and three-fourths (¾) of an inch from the top; the others eight (8) inches apart; a white-metal button below each button-hole, three and one-fourth (3¼) inches from the top. The sides of each half tent to have seven (7) buttons and button-holes; the side button-holes to be worked one (1) inch from the edge, the first to be nine (9) inches from the top, the others spaced eight (8) inches apart, and the buttons firmly sewed on four (4) inches from the edge. Each half tent to be furnished with a guy-line and three (3) foot-stops, made of six (6) thread manila line, small; the former six (6) feet long and the latter sixteen (16) inches long, all whipped at both ends. All sewing, including button-holes, to be done with W. B. linen thread, No. 70.

The shelter tents (halves) to conform in all respects to the standard sample.

Adopted January 18, 1889.

S. B. HOLABIRD,
Quartermaster General, U. S. A.

202—F., 1889.

280

SHELTER TENT
AND POLE

5 FT 6 IN

5' 5"

POLE & SOCKET

4"

4'

WAR DEPARTMENT,

Quartermaster General's Office.

Specifications for Iron Bedstead, with Woven-wire Bunk Bottom.

Iron Frames.—To consist of head and foot parts made of wrought-iron butt weld pipe, three-quarters (¾) of an inch inside diameter, bent to form of standard sample. Head part to stand three (3) feet three and one-half (3½) inches high from the floor. Foot part to stand two (2) feet nine and three-quarter (9¾) inches high from the floor. Width, two (2) feet six (6) inches inside. Iron knobs in bottom of posts, milled down to fit inside of pipe, and pinned entirely through pipe and knob. Castors of Philadelphia pattern, No. 7, with iron horn and iron wheel driven into knobs. One cross rod extending across head and foot parts, of one-half (½) inch round iron, milled down to a shoulder, running through the pipe and riveted down. "**T**" mosquito rods of one-half (½) inch round iron, three (3) feet one and one-half (1½) inches high, with arms two (2) feet six and one-half (6½) inches long, of three-eighths (⅜) inch round iron, connected at intersecting points by malleable iron tee, and connected at bottom with cross rod by iron tee, with thread cut on inside of tee and on outside of rod to allow the rod to be screwed in. To have corrugated iron strips (twelve and three-quarter (12¾) inches long, containing ten (10) interstices) riveted to outside of posts for connecting woven-wire bunk bottom with iron frames; or other device equally as good, and sanctioned by the contracting officer.

Woven-wire Bunk Bottom.—To consist of hard-maple frame, with side-rails six (6) feet six (6) inches long, three (3) inches wide, one and three-quarter (1¾) inches thick. End rails of same material, two (2) feet five and one-quarter (5¼) inches long, three (3) inches wide, one and three-quarter (1¾) inches thick, bolted together at each corner with one carriage-bolt three-eighths (⅜) of an inch diameter, five (5) inches long, with iron corner plates at each corner, screwed to frame with two (2) wood-screws one and three-quarter (1¾) inches, number 15, at top, and two (2) wood-screws one (1) inch, number 15, at bottom. Stretcher-bar (to increase and diminish tension of woven-wire fabric) of hard maple, one and three-quarter (1¾) inches by one and one-half (1½) inches, connected with end rail at foot of bedstead by three (3) square-head machine-bolts one-half (½) inch diameter, eight (8) inches long, threaded three (3) inches. Woven-wire fabric of double weaving, number 20 steel wire, of three-quarter ($\frac{3}{4}$) inch pitch, with three (3) strengthening coils on each outer edge, and four (4) strengthening coils distributed at equal distances apart, in body of wire fabric, to give additional strength. Woven-wire fabric fastened to end rail and stretcher-bar with eight (8) ounce carpet-tacks or double-pointed tacks, and held in place by half-round strips of hard maple one-half ($\frac{1}{2}$) inch thick, fastened with barbed-wire nails, and the crevices well puttied.

The woven-wire bunk bottom to be connected with head and foot posts at each corner by one hook-bolt (seven-sixteenths ($\frac{7}{16}$) of an inch diameter and threaded one (1) inch on end, and fitted with nut to tighten) to pass through iron corner plate and side rail, and bent to fit around corrugated strip on posts; or other device equally as good, and sanctioned by the contracting officer.

One wrench (to fit bolts) to be furnished with every two (2) bedsteads.

All wood used to be well seasoned, and to have a heavy coat of coach varnish of good quality.

All iron work to have a heavy coat of black varnish.

Adopted January 23, 1889.

S. B. HOLABIRD,
Quartermaster General, U. S. A.

228—F., 1889.

IRON BEDSTEAD
WITH WOVEN-WIRE BUNK BOTTOM.

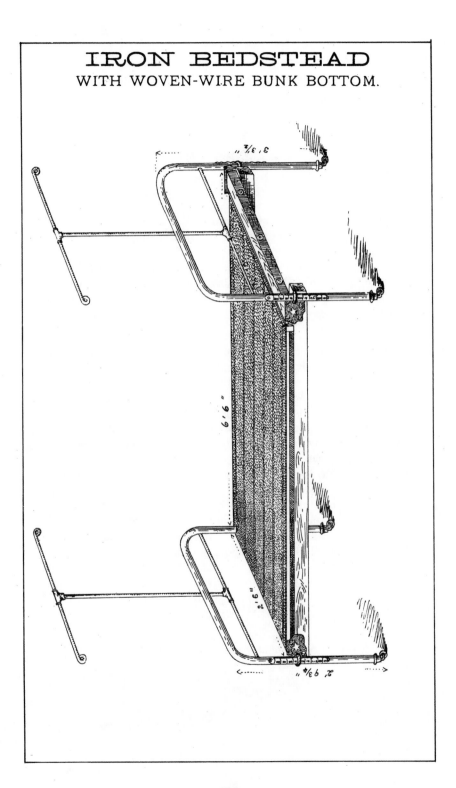

Specifications for Canvas Leggins.

Material.—To be made of regular standard fifteen (15) ounce cotton duck, dyed a brown color to shade of standard sample.

Measurements.—To be made in three (3) sizes, and numbered 1, 2, and 3. No. 3, the largest, to be not less than twelve (12) inches high when finished, fifteen (15) inches in width at the top, twelve and one-half (12½) inches at ankle, seventeen (17) inches from heel to toe. The measurements to be one-half (½) inch less for No. 2 and seven-eighths (⅞) inch less for No. 1.

Workmanship.—Seams to be not less than one-fourth (¼) inch wide, stayed on the inside with good quality one-half (½) inch shoe-stay webbing, stitched on each edge with No. 30 cotton. Top and bottom edges to be faced with same quality material, five-eighths (⅝) inch wide, with double row of stitching of same number of cotton. The front piece to be faced on the inside along its edge with five-eighths (⅝) inch shoe-stay binding, and to be fitted with seven (7) one-fourth (¼) inch grommets placed at equal distances. The back piece to be reinforced on the inside with a strip of best quality tanned horse-hide one (1) inch wide, and to be fitted with six (6) long brass studs placed at equal distances and firmly clinched. The leggins to fasten with a braided cotton cord running through the grommets and around the studs. An eyelet to be placed at the bottom of back-piece of the leggins where the lacing starts, and a grommet at the top to fasten the end of the cord. To have a strap at bottom of horse-hide leather about seven and one-half (7½) inches long, fastened on the inside of leggin by stitching and two (2) copper rivets, and the outside by means of a buckle; three (3) holes to be punched on end of strap to receive tongue of buckle.

Finish.—To conform in all respects to the sealed standard samples.

Adopted February 7, 1889, in lieu of specifications of January 10, 1888, which are hereby canceled.

S. B. HOLABIRD,
Quartermaster General, U. S. A.

360—F., 1889.

286

CANVAS LEGGINS.

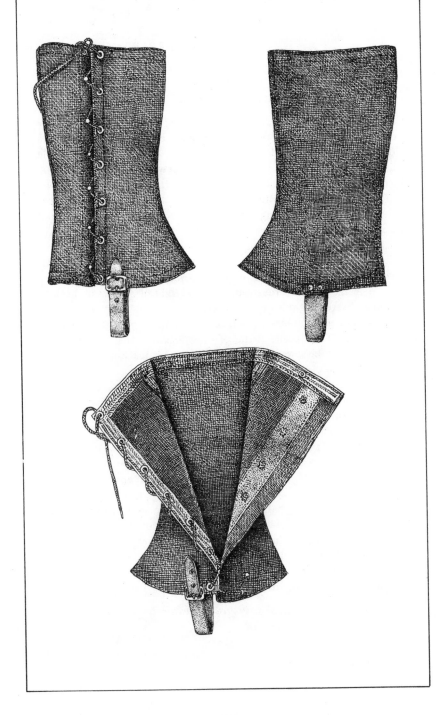

Specifications for Barrack Shoes.

Upper.—The upper to be made of a single piece of best quality sixteen (16) ounce (to twenty-eight and one-half (28½) inches width) cotton duck dyed brown. Quarters to be made of a double thickness, with sole-leather counter placed between. The vamp to be lined with heavy drilling. The vamp to have a tip over the toe, to be made of russet calfskin with grain side out; to be stitched to upper with two rows of stitching slightly apart to allow room for small punch-holes. The top of vamp to be covered with same material, in order to give additional strength where eyelets are inserted, the same to be lined with sheepskin. The sock-lining to be of same material. All seams to be stayed on the inside with webbing. The canvas to be lasted over the toe, underneath the tip. Height of quarter at back to be two and seven-eighths (2⅞) inches.

Sole.—The insole, outsole, and heel to be made of first quality oak sole-leather. The outsole to be of one thickness, that is, no slip or tap sole, and to be sewed by the McKay sewing machine; stitches to be covered by a channel on the outsole.

Measurements (*Last*).—Size, 8. Length on bottom, eleven (11) inches. Width on bottom across ball, three and one-fourth (3¼) inches. Width on bottom across heel, two and one-half (2½) inches. Width on bottom across shank, two (2) inches. Heel measure, thirteen and one-fourth (13¼) inches. Instep, nine and seven-eighths (9⅞) inches. Ball, nine and three-eighths (9⅜) inches.

Measurements (*Shoe*).—Outside measurements after shoe is made. Length of sole over all, eleven and one-fourth (11¼) inches. Width of sole, ball, three and one-half (3½) inches. Width of heel, two and one-half (2½) inches. Length of heel, two and three-fourths (2¾) inches. Height of heel, one (1) inch. Other sizes to be made in proportion.

Quality.—All materials to be of the best quality, and all to be put together in a first-class and workmanlike manner. Each pair of shoes to be furnished with a pair of half (½) yard *heavy iron laces.*

Adopted February 7, 1889, *in lieu of specifications of February* 26, 1887, *which are hereby canceled.*

S. B. HOLABIRD,

Quartermaster General, U, S. A.

360—F., 1889.

BARRACK SHOES.

0   3"   6"

Specifications for Fur Campaign Hats.

Mixture.—To be composed of fur in the following proportions and kinds, for twenty-four (24) dozen hats: Fifteen (15) pounds Y. C. Ex. Ex. coney; thirty (30) pounds Y. C. No. 1 coney; sixteen (16) pounds W. C. No. 1 coney; twelve (12) pounds W. C. mottled coney; five (5) pounds W. C. hare's bellies; ten (10) pounds blown nutria; ten (10) pounds American rabbit.

Weight.—Hat bodies to be weighed, four and three-fourths (4¾) ounces heavy.

Shape.—Block to be five and three-fourths (5¾) inches deep to center of tip.

Brim.—To be two and three-fourths (2¾) inches wide in front and rear, and three (3) inches at sides; and to have three rows of stitching on edge.

Color.—To be drab, shade of standard sample.

Trimmings.—To be trimmed with eight-ligne union band, same quality and style as on hat, to be sewed on by hand. Sweat to be an imported lined leather, two and one-fourth (2¼) inches wide, sewed to the reed by zigzag stitch. Each side of hat to have an opening for ventilation consisting of small punched holes of size, and arranged in design, as on standard sample hat; the center of design to be about three and one-quarter (3¼) inches from brim.

The hats to be doe-finished, as per sample.

To be packed three hats in each band-box.

Adopted February 8, 1889, *in lieu of specifications of December* 14, 1883, *which are hereby canceled.*

S. B. HOLABIRD,
Quartermaster General, U. S. A.

371—F., 1889.

290

CAMPAIGN HAT
FOR ENLISTED MEN.

SIDE VIEW

FRONT VIEW

WAR DEPARTMENT,

Quartermaster General's Office.

Specifications for Helmets, untrimmed, for all Troops.

Material.—To be made of felt composed of two-fifths ($\frac{2}{5}$) yellow carroted double ring I H Russia, two-fifths ($\frac{2}{5}$) yellow carroted best coney backs, and one-fifth ($\frac{1}{5}$) best colored muskrat.

Small sizes to be formed on cone 25 by 27 inches, and each body to weigh three and one-eighth ($3\frac{1}{8}$) ounces.

Large sizes to be formed on cone 26 by 28 inches, and each body to weigh three and three-eighths ($3\frac{3}{8}$) ounces.

Helmets to be wine stiffened and to have a "long" black color. Suitable holes must be made in the sides of the helmet for fastening on the side buttons.

Shape, etc.—To be in shape according to the standard sample. Black enameled leather band, seven-eighths ($\frac{7}{8}$) of an inch wide, to surround the helmet at the base of the crown, and to have an adjustable chin-strap, each part ten and one-half ($10\frac{1}{2}$) inches long, of the same material, with brass sliding buckle, as on sample. The lower edge of helmet to be bound with black enameled leather, and the inside of visor all around to be lined with green morocco leather, pasted to the body with rubber cement. The sweat-leather to be of Belgian sheep-skin two (2) inches wide; inside the sweat-leather a band one (1) inch wide, of heavy enameled leather. All to be well stitched to place.

Sizes.—To be of six (6) standard sizes, numbered from one (1) to six (6), inclusive, corresponding to the trade sizes, $6\frac{3}{4}$ to $7\frac{3}{8}$, inclusive.

The standard sample to be followed in all respects as to shape, quality of materials, workmanship, etc.

Adopted February 12, 1889, in lieu of specifications approved January 13, 1888, which are hereby canceled.

S. B. HOLABIRD,

Quartermaster General, U. S. A.

398—F., 1889.

HELMET,
UNTRIMMED.

HELMET.
FOOT.

HELMET,
MOUNTED

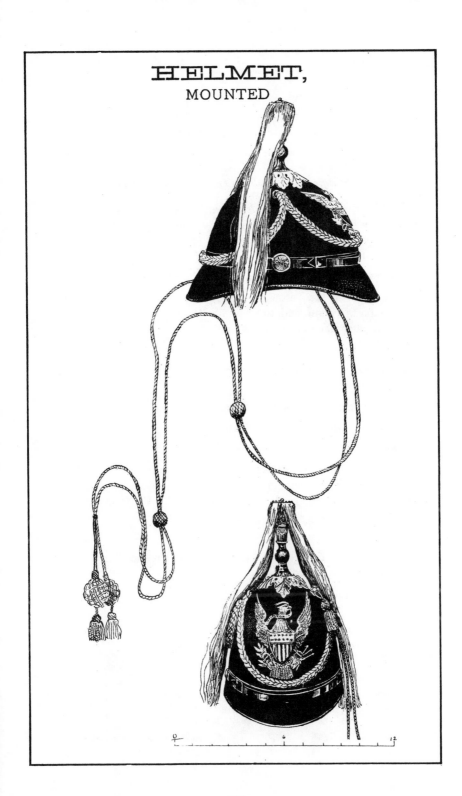

Specifications for Boots (hand-sewed bottoms).

Materials.—*Vamp and outside counter* to be of the best oak-tanned wax upper leather, from slaughter hides, weighing not less than six and one-half (6½) nor more than seven (7) ounces to the square foot when in the whole side.

Inside counter to be of oak-tanned slaughter leather.

Legs to be of the best oak-tanned leather from slaughter hides, finished on the grain, and to weigh not less than seven (7) ounces to the square foot when in the whole side.

Straps to be of calfskin or smooth wax upper leather.

Inner soles to be of best oak-tanned whole leather; no split leather to be used.

Welts to be of pure oak-tanned slaughter leather.

Shank-pieces to be of oak sole-leather.

Bottom filling to be of oak wax upper leather.

Out-soles to be of best oak-tanned leather made from straight Texas or South American (commonly called "Spanish") dry hides, and to be cut from overweight, plump, full-shouldered sides, running from twenty (20) to twenty-four (24) pounds to the side.

Thread to be of the best quality silk and linen.

Nails to be of best quality Swede iron and American iron of the sizes hereinafter specified.

Sizes.—To run from 5 to 12, inclusive, and to be of letters "A," "B," and "C" widths.

Measurements.—The width of the soles across the ball of the foot to be as follows, and to be in proportion throughout:

SIZES.	5	6	7	8	9	10	11	12
Letter "A"	$3\frac{5}{16}$	$3\frac{7}{16}$	$3\frac{9}{16}$	$3\frac{11}{16}$	$3\frac{13}{16}$	$3\frac{15}{16}$	$4\frac{1}{16}$	$4\frac{3}{16}$
Letter "B"	$3\frac{3}{8}$	$3\frac{1}{2}$	$3\frac{5}{8}$	$3\frac{3}{4}$	$3\frac{7}{8}$	4	$4\frac{1}{8}$	$4\frac{1}{4}$
Letter "C"	$3\frac{7}{16}$	$3\frac{9}{16}$	$3\frac{11}{16}$	$3\frac{13}{16}$	$3\frac{15}{16}$	$4\frac{1}{16}$	$4\frac{3}{16}$	$4\frac{5}{16}$

The instep and ball to measure as follows:

SIZES.	5		6		7		8		9		10		11		12	
	Instep.	Ball.	Instep.	Ball.	Instep.	Ball.	Instep.	Ball.	Instep.	Ball.	Instep.	Ball.	Instep.	Ball.	Instep.	Ball.
Letter "A"	8¾	8½	9	8¾	9¼	9	9½	9¼	9¾	9½	10	9¾	10¼	10	10½	10¼
Letter "B"	9	8¾	9¼	9	9½	9¼	9¾	9½	10	9¾	10¼	10	10½	10¼	10¾	10½
Letter "C"	9¼	9	9½	9¼	9¾	9½	10	9¾	10¼	10	10½	10¼	10¾	10½	11	10¾

Measurement for a No. 8 boot, standard Letter "A," to be as follows: *Ball or toe,* nine and one-fourth (9¼) inches; *instep,* nine and one-half (9½) inches; *heel,* thirteen and three-fourths (13¾) inches; *length of leg* to measure from the inside shank nineteen (19) inches in front and fourteen (14) inches in back above the heel; *width of leg* at top to be sixteen and one-half (16½) inches; *width of strap,* one and one-fourth (1¼) inches; *length of strap,* seven (7) inches; *height of counter,* three (3) inches; *width of heel,* two and three-fourths (2¾) inches; *length of heel,* two and seven-eighths (2⅞) inches; *height of heel,* one and one-fourth (1¼) inches; *width of sole* across ball, three and eleven-sixteenths (3¹¹⁄₁₆) inches.

Measurement for a No. 8 boot, standard Letter "B," to be as Letter "A," with the following exceptions:

Ball or toe, nine and one-half (9½) inches; *instep,* nine and three-fourths (9¾) inches; *heel,* fourteen (14) inches; *width of leg* at top, sixteen and three-fourths (16¾) inches; *width of sole* across ball, three and three-fourths (3¾) inches.

Measurement for a No. 8 boot, standard Letter "C," to be as Letter "A," with the following exceptions:

Ball or toe, nine and three-fourths (9¾) inches; *instep,* ten (10) inches; *heel,* fourteen and one-fourth (14¼) inches; *width of leg* at top, seventeen (17) inches; *width of sole* across ball, three and thirteen-sixteenths (3¹³⁄₁₆) inches.

Length of leg to increase one-fourth (¼) inch on each size above No. 8 and decrease one-fourth (¼) inch on each size below.

Width of leg at top to increase one-fourth (¼) inch on each size, and letter of same, above No. 8, and decrease one-fourth (¼) inch on each size, and letter of same, below.

Heel measure to increase one-fourth (¼) inch on each size, and letter of same, above No. 8, and decrease one-fourth (¼) inch on each size, and letter of same, below.

Workmanship and finish.—The *leg* to be cut in two (2) pieces, seams to lap over three-eighths (⅜) inch and stitched with three (3) rows of stitching, ten (10) stitches to the inch; the upper thread to be best quality Belding Bros. & Co. silk, Letter " E " or " EE," or other equally as good; the under thread to be of No. 25 best quality of Marshall's linen thread, or other equally as good; *back* to be seamed on outside and to be covered with strip of same material as the leg, to measure one (1) inch in width at top and two (2) inches in width at counter, and to be stitched with five (5) cord waxed linen thread, six (6) stitches to the inch. *Vamp* and *outside counter* to be stitched ten (10) stitches to the inch, the upper thread to be of best quality Belding Bros. & Co. silk, Letter " E " or " EE," or other equally as good; the under thread to be of best quality No. 25 Marshall's linen thread or other equally as good. The *strap* to be sewed to the inside of the leg with five (5) cord waxed linen thread, six (6) stitches to the inch. The *inner sole* to be worked square with the last and "stump-feathered." The *inner sole, welt,* and *upper* to be fastened together with ten (10) cord No. 10 waxed sole-thread, four (4) stitches to the inch. The *outer sole* and *welt* to be fastened together with nine (9) cord No. 10 waxed sole-thread, six (6) to seven (7) stitches to the inch. All thread used to be properly waxed and stitches well drawn up. The *outer sole* not to be channeled.

Lift to be put under the sole of heel-seat corresponding to welt, and to be nailed with ⅞ 14-wire Swede nails, four (4) to the inch, and, when the heel is built up ready for top piece, to be nailed with ⅝ 14-wire Swede nails, three (3) to the inch. The *top piece* to be nailed around with ⅝ overstout iron nails, four (4) to the inch, with the addition of a half row on the outside of heel and three (3) ⅝ nails, overstout, on the breast of heel.

The *soles* to be finished without removing grain on leather. The edges of soles to be made square-set and burnished with irons without heel-ball. Size and letter to be stamped on sole of each boot, which is to measure one size more than marked.

Lasts.—The *lasts* to be used to be subject to the approval of the contracting officer.

Adopted February 20, 1889.

S. B. HOLABIRD,
Quartermaster General, U. S. A.

391—F., 1889.

BOOTS,

SEWED.

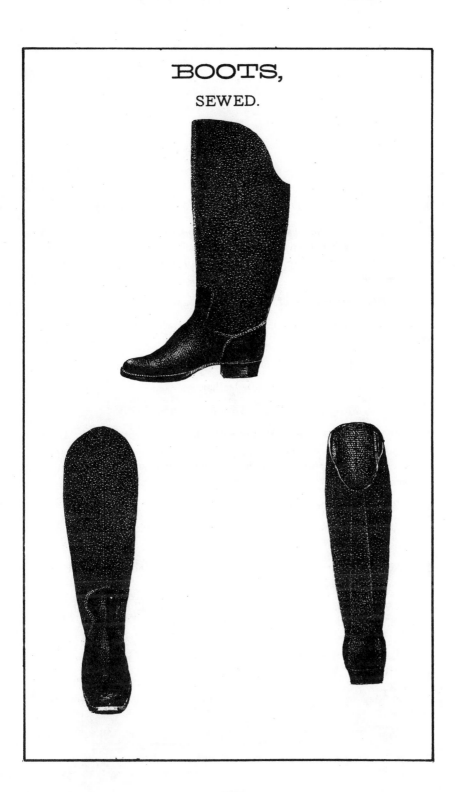

Specifications for Campaign Shoes (hand-sewed bottoms).

Materials.—*Vamp, quarter, and long counter* to be of best oak-tanned wax upper leather, from slaughter hides, weighing not less than six and one-half (6½) nor more than seven (7) ounces to the square foot when in the whole side.

Middle counter to be of oak-tanned slaughter leather.

Inner soles to be of the best oak-tanned whole leather. No split leather to be used.

Welts to be of pure oak-tanned slaughter leather.

Shank pieces to be of oak sole leather.

Bottom filling to be of oak wax upper leather.

Out-soles to be of best oak-tanned leather, made from straight Texas or South American (commonly called "Spanish") dry hides, and to be cut from over-weight, plump, full-shouldered sides, running from twenty (20) to twenty-four (24) pounds to the side.

Thread to be best quality linen.

Nails to be best quality Swede iron and American iron, of the sizes hereinafter specified.

Sizes.—To run from Nos. 5 to 12, inclusive, and to be of Letter "A," "B," and "C" widths.

Measurements.—The width of soles across the ball of the foot to be as follows, and to be in proportion throughout :

SIZES.	5	6	7	8	9	10	11	12
	"	"	"	"	"	"	"	"
Letter "A"	3 5/16	3 7/16	3 9/16	3 11/16	3 13/16	3 15/16	4 1/16	4 3/16
Letter "B"	3⅜	3½	3⅝	3¾	3⅞	4	4⅛	4¼
Letter "C"	3 7/16	3 9/16	3 11/16	3 13/16	3 15/16	4 1/16	4 3/16	4 5/16

The *instep and ball* to measure as follows :

SIZES.	5		6		7		8		9		10		11		12	
	Instep	Ball	Instep	Ball	Instep	Ball	Instep	Ball	Instep	Ball	Instep	Ball	Instep	Ball	Instep	Ball
	"	"	"	"	"	"	"	"	"	"	"	"	"	"	"	"
Letter "A"	8¾	8½	9	8¾	9¼	9	9½	9¼	9¾	9½	10	9¾	10¼	10	10½	10¼
Letter "B"	9	8¾	9¼	9	9½	9¼	9¾	9½	10	9¾	10¼	10	10½	10¼	10¾	10½
Letter "C"	9¼	9	9½	9¼	9¾	9½	10	9¾	10¼	10	10½	10¼	10¾	10½	11	10¾

Measurements for a No. 8 *shoe,* standard, *Letter "A,"* to be as follows : *Heel* 13⅛ inches, *instep* 9½ inches, *ball or toe* 9¼ inches, *height of back at rear* 5½ inches, *length of heel* 3 inches, *width of heel* 2⅞ inches, *height of heel* 1⅛ inches, *width of sole or ball* 3$\frac{11}{16}$ inches.

Measurements for a No. 8 *shoe,* standard, *Letter "B,"* to be as Letter "A," with the following exceptions: *Heel* 13⅜ inches, *instep* 9¾ inches, *ball or toe* 9½ inches, *width of sole or ball* 3¾ inches.

Measurements for a No. 8 *shoe,* standard, *Letter "C,"* to be as Letter "A," with the following exceptions: *Heel* 13⅝ inches, *instep* 10 inches, *ball or toe* 9¾ inches, *width of sole or ball* 3$\frac{13}{16}$ inches.

Heel measure to increase one-fourth (¼) inch on each size, and letter of same, above No. 8, and decrease one-fourth (¼) inch on each size, and letter of same below.

Height of quarter at rear to increase one-eighth (⅛) inch on each size above No. 8, and decrease one-eighth (⅛) inch on each size below.

Workmanship and finish.—Vamp and quarter to be crimped ; top of vamp to be neatly skived down three (3) inches. Long counter to be neatly skived on the grain side around the upper edge and fastened to the quarter with three (3) cord No. 16 waxed linen thread, nine (9) stitches to the inch. Middle counter to be neatly skived. The inner sole to be worked square with the last and "stump-feathered." The inner sole, upper, and welt to be fastened together with ten (10) cord No. 10 wax sole thread, four (4) stitches to the inch. Outer sole and welt to be fastened together with nine (9) cord No. 10 wax sole thread, six (6) to seven (7) stitches to the inch.

All thread used to be properly waxed and stitches well drawn up. The outer sole not to be channeled.

Lift to be put under the sole of heel-seat corresponding to welt, and to be nailed with ⅞ 14-wire Swede nails, four (4) to the inch, and when the heel is built up ready for top piece to be nailed with $\frac{8}{8}$ 14-wire Swede nails, three (3) to the inch. The top piece to be nailed around with $\frac{9}{8}$ over-stout iron nails, four (4) to the inch, with the addition of a half row on the outside of heel, and three $\frac{8}{8}$ nails, over-stout, on the breast of heel.

The heel seat to be neatly lined with 8-ounce cotton duck, securely pasted to the inner sole. The soles to be finished without removing grain on leather.

The edges of soles to be made square, set and burnished with irons without heel-ball. Size and letter to be stamped on sole of each shoe, which is to measure one size more than marked.

Each shoe to be finished with three (3) hooks of standard size, and from five (5) to six (6) eyelets, standard size, on each side, according to size of shoe. Each pair of shoes to be furnished with a pair of tipped pospoise laces of best quality, thirty-six (36) inches long.

Lasts.—The lasts to be used to be subject to the approval of the contracting officer.

Adopted February 20, 1889.

S. B. HOLABIRD,
Quartermaster General, U. S. A.

391—F., 1889.

CAMPAIGN SHOES.

WAR DEPARTMENT,
QUARTERMASTER GENERAL'S OFFICE.

Specifications for Tripods (for conical Wall-tent).

Tripod to consist of a cast-iron pole-socket two (2) inches deep and about two and one-eighth (2⅛) inches in diameter inside, having at equal distance on outside three (3) projecting double brackets to receive the legs. The legs, three (3) in number, to be made of three (3) inch by one-eighth (⅛) inch wrought iron, bent into semi-tubular form toward the outside; the upper end to have an extra piece of the same iron inserted, making three (3) thicknesses welded together, for about three (3) inches, so as to enter the brackets. The lower ends to be turned back one-half (½) inch, forming feet to the tripod. Length of legs from feet when finished four (4) feet six (6) inches. A staple to be securely fixed in bottom of the socket, from which depends a chain eighteen (18) inches long (containing thirty-one links) and a pot hook two and one-half (2½) inches, on which to hang cooking utensils, an extra "**S**" hook about one and one-half (1½) inches long in the upper link of this chain.

Adopted February 27, 1889.

S. B. HOLABIRD,
Quartermaster General, U. S. A.

519—F., 1889.

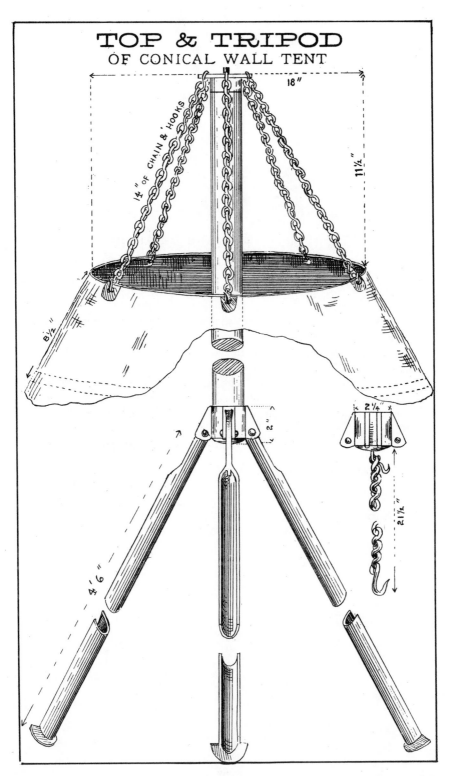

TOP & TRIPOD
OF CONICAL WALL TENT

18"

11½"

14" OF CHAIN & HOOKS

8½

2"

2¼"

21½"

4'6"

WAR DEPARTMENT,

QUARTERMASTER GENERAL'S OFFICE.

Specifications for White Jeans—Bleached.

To be full twenty-seven (27) inches wide, and free from imperfections.

To contain seventy-two (72) threads to the inch of warp and forty-six (46) threads to the inch of filling.

To weigh not less than four and three-fourths (4¾) ounces to the linear yard, and be capable of sustaining a strain of seventy-six (76) pounds to the inch of warp and forty-four (44) pounds to the inch of filling.

To be equal in quality, weave, and finish to the standard sample.

Adopted March 27, 1889.

S. B. HOLABIRD,
Quartermaster General, U. S. A.

790—F., 1889.

Specifications for 6½ to 7-ounce Cotton Duck (Unbleached).

Cotton.—To be American cotton of grade not inferior to "Low Middling."

Width.—To be full twenty-eight and one-half (28½) inches when finished.

Threads.—To contain not less than fifty-two (52) threads of warp and forty-eight (48) threads of filling to the square inch.

Weight.—To weigh not less than six and one-half (6½) ounces to the linear yard.

Strength.—To be capable of sustaining a strain of seventy-two (72) pounds in the warp and thirty (30) pounds in the filling to the one-half (½) inch, tested in the piece.

Workmanship, weave, and finish.—To be woven in a workmanlike manner, free from imperfections; to be entirely free from sizing, and not to be "hot-finished;" to be without the blue stripes usually woven in cotton duck; to be as free from specks, seeds, or oil stains as the standard sample, and in quality and size of yarn, weave, and finish to conform to said sample.

Adopted March 28, 1889.

S. B. HOLABIRD,
Quartermaster General, U. S. A.

814—F., 1889.

307

WAR DEPARTMENT,

QUARTERMASTER GENERAL'S OFFICE.

Specifications for 6½ to 7-ounce Cotton Duck (Bleached).

Cotton.—To be American cotton of grade not inferior to "Low Middling."

Width.—To be full twenty-eight and one-half (28½) inches when finished.

Threads.—To contain not less than fifty-two (52) threads of warp and forty-eight (48) threads of filling to the square inch.

Weight.—To weigh not less than six and one-half (6½) ounces to the linear yard.

Strength.—To be capable of sustaining a strain of fifty-six (56) pounds in the warp and twenty-eight (28) pounds in the filling to the one-half (½) inch, tested in the piece.

Workmanship, weave, color, and finish.—To be woven in a workmanlike manner, free from imperfections; to be entirely free from sizing and not to be "hot finished;" to be without the blue stripes usually woven in cotton duck; to be as free from specks, seeds, or oil stains as the standard sample, and in quality and size of yarn, weave, finish, and color to conform to said sample.

Adopted March 28, 1889.

S. B. HOLABIRD,
Quartermaster General, U. S. A.

814—F., 1889.

WAR DEPARTMENT,

QUARTERMASTER GENERAL'S OFFICE.

Specifications for 6½ to 7-ounce Cotton Duck (dyed brown).

Cotton.—To be American cotton of grade not inferior to "Low Middling."

Width.—To be full twenty-eight-and one-half (28½) inches when finished.

Threads.—To contain not less than fifty-two (52) threads of warp and forty-eight (48) threads of filling to the square inch.

Weight.—To weigh not less than six and one-half (6½) ounces to the linear yard.

Strength.—To be capable of sustaining a strain of seventy (70) pounds in the warp and thirty (30) pounds in the filling to the one-half inch tested in the piece.

Workmanship, weave, finish, and color.—To be woven in a workmanlike manner, free from imperfections; to be entirely free from sizing, and not to be "hot finished;" to be without the blue stripes usually woven in cotton duck; to be as free from specks, seeds, or oil stains as the standard sample, and in quality and size of yarn, weave, finish, and color to conform to said sample.

Adopted March 28, 1889.

S. B. HOLABIRD,
Quartermaster General, U. S. A.

814—F., 1889.

WAR DEPARTMENT,
QUARTERMASTER GENERAL'S OFFICE

Specifications for Overalls.

Material.—To be made of six and one-half (6½) to seven (7) ounce cotton duck, unbleached, twenty-eight and one-half (28½) inches wide.

Pattern for Engineers.—To consist of two parts, a body or jacket and a pair of trowsers. The body loose, without yoke, slightly gathered at waist-band, opening at back, and fastening at top with two (2) buttons and at waist with strap and strong brass buckle, the strap being a continuation of the waist-band. Sleeves loose, with narrow cuff-band to button. Waist-band about one and three-quarter (1¾) inches wide, and to have six (6) button-holes placed so as to suit the suspender buttons upon the trowsers, and one button-hole in the center of front to receive the top button on the front of the waist-band of the same.

The lower part to be in form of a loose pair of trowsers, with waist-band; two (2) white metal buttons on front of waist-band, and same kind of buttons placed in proper position for use with suspenders. No covered fly. One button on center of fly opening.

For Mounted Men, and also for Summer Use by Non-commissioned Officers and Privates of all Arms.—To be the same as the lower or trowsers part of those for engineers.

MEASUREMENTS.

	No. 1.	No. 2.	No. 3.	No. 4.	No. 5.
JACKET.	*Inches.*	*Inches.*	*Inches.*	*Inches.*	*Inches.*
Breast measure	38	39	41	43	45
Waist	34	35	37	39	42
Collar	17	18	18½	19	20
Length of sleeve	32½	33	33½	34	35
Length of body	18	18½	19	19½	21
TROWSERS.					
Outside seam	42	43	44	45	46
Inside seam	31	32	33	34	35
Waist	32	34	36	38	40
Bottom	20	20	20½	20½	21

Adopted June 21, 1889, in lieu of specifications of March 12, 1879, and September 22, 1888, which are hereby canceled.

S. B. HOLABIRD,
Quartermaster General, U. S. A.

1707—F., 1889.

310

OVERALLS
ENGINEERS.

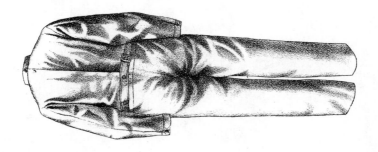

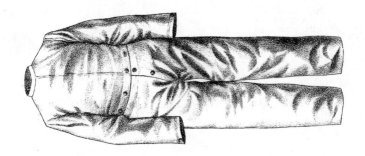

OVERALLS
FOR MOUNTED MEN
AND ALSO FOR SUMMER USE BY NON-COMMISSIONED OFFICERS AND PRIVATES OF ALL ARMS

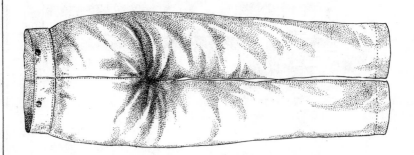

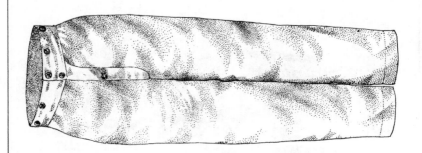

WAR DEPARTMENT,

QUARTERMASTER GENERAL'S OFFICE.

Specifications for Books of Record.

Regimental Order Book.—To be made of paper equal in quality to the standard sample. Leaves eleven (11) inches by sixteen (16) inches, faint-lined, paged; two hundred and sixty-four (264) pages, with marbled edges, full bound in smooth sheepskin binding, with Russia-leather ends and center strap, patent spring back, with title lettered and finished in gold, and four (4) raised bands. The joints to be muslin-lined, and the fly-leaves next the cover to be of marbled paper; two (2) additional fly-leaves on each side.

Regimental Letters-Received Book.—To be the same as above, with the addition of ruled and printed headings, as per sample; and each book to be supplied with a printed copy of instructions, as per sample, pasted on the inside of the front cover.

Regimental Letters-Sent Book.—To be the same as the Regimental Order Book, except that it is to have a marginal line, and printed instructions on the inside of front cover, as per sample.

Index to Regimental Letters-Received Book.—Leaves to be eleven (11) inches by sixteen (16) inches, full bound in rough sheepskin binding, to be faint and marginal lined and marble edges. To contain twenty-six (26) leaves, properly indexed, and to have a side title, lettered and finished in gold, similar to the standard sample, and printed instructions pasted on the inside of the front cover.

Index to Regimental Letters-Sent Book.—To be the same as the next above, except as to the title.

Post Order Book.—To be made of paper equal in quality to the standard sample. Leaves eleven (11) inches by sixteen (16) inches, faint-lined, paged; two hundred and sixty-four (264) pages, with marbled edges, full bound in smooth sheepskin binding, with Russia-leather ends and center strap, patent spring back, with title lettered and finished in gold, and four raised bands. The joints to be muslin-lined, and the fly-leaves next the cover to be of marble paper and to have two (2) additional fly-leaves on each side.

Post Council of Administration Record Book.—To be the same as next above except as to title.

Post Letters-Received Book.—To be full bound, as described for Regimental Order Book; leaves eleven (11) inches by sixteen (16) inches, paged; two hundred and sixty-four (264) pages, faint-lined, printed and ruled headings, as per sample; printed instructions pasted on inside of front cover.

Post Letters-Sent Book.—Same as next above as to size, binding, paging, and number of pages, but to be faint-lined, with marginal line, marbled edges, and printed instructions pasted on the inside of the front cover.

Index to Post Letters-Received Book.—Same as Index to Regimental Letters-Received Book, except as to the title.

Index to Post Letters-Sent Book.—To be the same as next above, except as to the title.

Company Letters-Received Book.—To be made of paper in quality and size the same as for Regimental Order Book; faint-lined, ruled, and printed headings, as per sample, paged; one hundred and seventy-six (176) pages; side title lettered and finished in gold, similar to sample; marbled edges, full bound in rough sheepskin binding, and to have printed instructions pasted on the inside of front cover.

Company Letters-Sent Book.—Same as next above as to size, paging, number of pages, binding, instructions, etc., but to be faint and margin lined only.

Index to Company Letters-Received Book and Index to Company Letters-Sent Book.—To be the same as described for Index to Regimental Letters-Received Book, except as to the titles.

Company Order Book.—To be made of the same size and quality of paper as the books hereinbefore described; faint-lined, paged; eighty-six (86) pages, marbled edges, and full bound in rough sheepskin binding, with side title lettered and finished in gold.

All of the above-specified books to be fully equal, in weight and quality of paper, binding, and finish, to the sealed standard samples.

Adopted July 19, 1889, *in lieu of specifications of January* 5, 1889, *which are hereby canceled.*

S. B. HOLABIRD,
Quartermaster General, U. S. A.

2128—F., 1889.

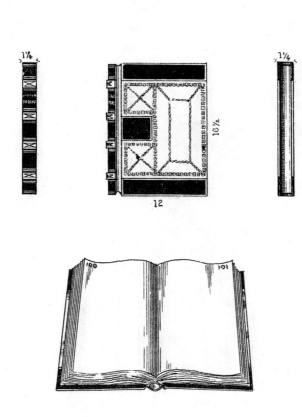

LETTERS RECEIVED
REGIMENTAL.

1¼

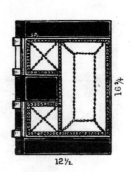

16¾

12½

1¼

LETTERS SENT
REGIMENTAL.

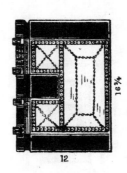

12

REGIMENTAL INDEX
OF LETTERS RECEIVED.

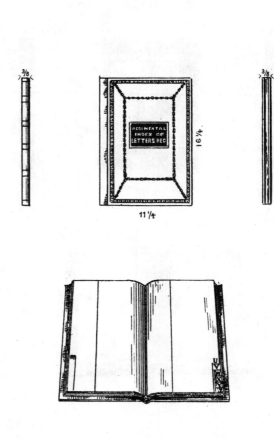

REGIMENTAL INDEX

OF LETTERS SENT.

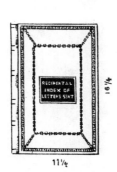

16½

11¼

⅜

⅜

REGIMENTAL
INDEX OF
LETTERS SENT

POST ORDERS.

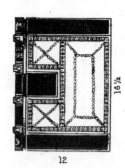

12

POST LETTERS
RECEIVED.

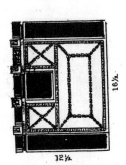

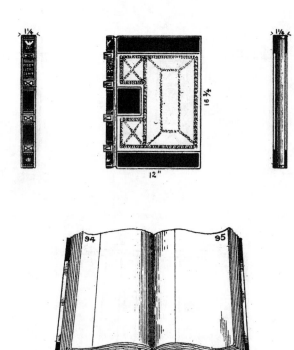

POST INDEX
OF LETTERS RECEIVED.

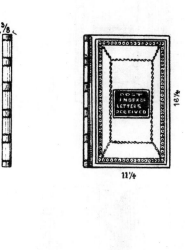

POST INDEX
OF LETTERS SENT.

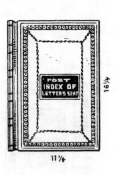

16¼

11¼

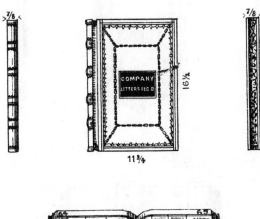

COMPANY LETTERS
SENT.

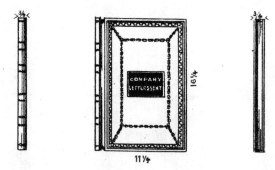

16¼

11¼

COMPANY INDEX
OF LETTERS RECEIVED

 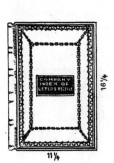 

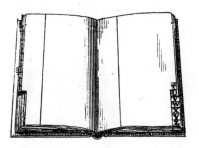

COMPANY INDEX
OF LETTERS SENT.

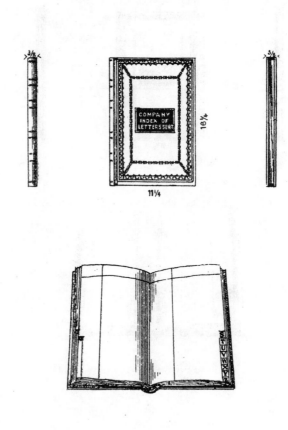

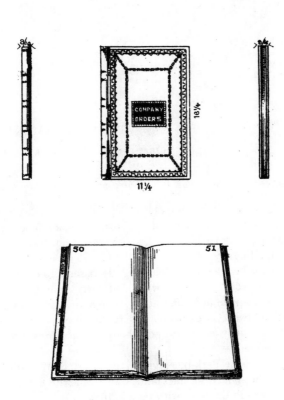

WAR DEPARTMENT,

QUARTERMASTER GENERAL'S OFFICE.

Specifications for Dark-blue Wool Shirting and Cape Lining Flannel.

To be fifty-four (54) inches, or $\frac{6}{4}$ wide, and to be made of pure long-staple American fleece wool, not less than one-half blood, free from shoddy, flocks, or other impurities, and to weigh not less than ten (10) ounces to the linear yard.

To be twilled and the nap very slightly raised; to contain not less than fifty-six (56) threads of warp and forty-eight (48) threads of filling in each square inch, and to be capable of sustaining a strain of not less than twenty-six (26) pounds to the inch in width of warp, and not less than twenty (20) pounds to the inch in width of filling, tested in the piece.

The colors to be dark-blue, green, gray, crimson, scarlet, yellow, and buff, of the standard shades, and to be dyed with fast colors. The blue to be dyed in the wool with pure indigo.

Adopted June 10, 1889, in lieu of those of April 18, 1888, which are hereby canceled.

S. B. HOLABIRD,
Quartermaster General, U. S. A.

1571—F., 1889.

330

WAR DEPARTMENT,

QUARTERMASTER GENERAL'S OFFICE.

Specifications for Facing Cloth.

To be fifty-four (54) inches or $\frac{6}{4}$ wide, of best fleece wool, free from shoddy, flocks, or other impurities.

To be dyed in the following colors, viz.: dark blue, scarlet, yellow, crimson, gray, emerald green, white, and buff.

To contain sixty-four (64) threads in the chain, sixty (60) threads in the filling to the square inch, and to weigh from fourteen and one-half (14½) to fifteen and one-half (15½) ounces to the linear yard, but not to fall below fourteen and one-half (14½) ounces.

To be capable of sustaining a strain of thirty (30) pounds to the inch in width of warp, and twenty (20) pounds to the inch in width of filling.

Adopted June 10, 1889, in lieu of specifications of March 26, 1885, which are hereby canceled.

S. B. HOLABIRD,
Quartermaster General, U. S. A.

1571—F., 1889.

WAR DEPARTMENT,

QUARTERMASTER GENERAL'S OFFICE.

Specifications for Overcoats.

Material.—Sky-blue kersey, twenty-two (22) ounce, Army standard. Lining for body, dark-blue flannel, to weigh thirteen (13) ounces to the $\frac{6}{4}$ lineal yard. Flannel for cape lining, Army standard, to weigh ten (10) ounces to the $\frac{6}{4}$ lineal yard, and to be of the following colors, viz.: For hospital stewards, emerald green; for post quartermaster sergeants, buff; for commissary sergeants, gray; for Ordnance, crimson; for Engineers and Artillery, scarlet; for Infantry, dark blue; for Cavalry, yellow. Sleeve lining, corset jeans. Eight (8) white metal hooks and eyes, large, viz.: Seven (7) for adjusting the cape to the coat, and one (1) on the collar; one (1) black japanned hook and eye at the bottom of front of skirt to hook it back, and four (4) black japanned hooks, two (2) on each edge, the upper hook placed eleven (11) inches below the lower button hole, and the lower hook thirteen (13) inches from the upper hook; four (4) worked eyes, two (2) on each side of the skirt, placed in position to hook up each front corner of the shirt at an angle which will show twelve (12) inches of the bottom of the skirt turned up.

Pattern.—To be double-breasted, with cape, and having six (6) regulation brass butttons, large, on each breast. Tne cape to be adjustable by means of seven (7) hooks beneath the collar of the coat, and seven (7) eyes upon the cape. To have seven (7) regulation brass buttons, small, one (1) inside pocket on the left breast, opening perpendicularly.

Workmanship.—To be cut and made in conformity with the standard patterns and samples.

SIZES.	Length of Coat.	Length of Cape.	Breast Measurement.	Waist Measurement.	Length of Sleeve.	Length of Collar.
1	44½	24½	36	34	32½	17
2	45	25½	38	36	33	17¼
3	46	26½	41	39	33½	18½
4	47	27½	44	42	34	19½
5	48	28½	45	44	34½	20
6	49	29	46	46	35	20½

Adopted June 10, 1889, in lieu of specifications of January 7, 1889, which are hereby cancelled.

S. B. HOLABIRD,
Quartermaster General, U. S. A.

1571—F., 1889.

332

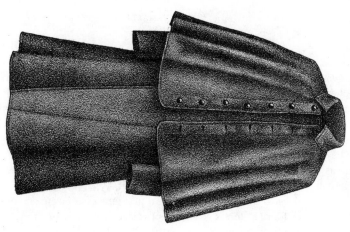

OVERCOAT.

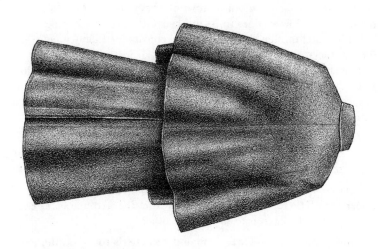

WAR DEPARTMENT,

QUARTERMASTER GENERAL'S OFFICE.

Specifications for Cloth Chevrons.

Cloth.—The cloth forming the groundwork for arms, arcs, and ties of chevrons to be of facing cloth (conforming to published specifications) of the same color as the facings of the uniform coat, except in the case of the Infantry overcoat chevron, when it will be of dark-blue cloth.

The cloth forming the groundwork for chevron devices to be the same as that for the uniform coat. For Pioneers and Farriers device to be cut about nine (9) by five and one-half (5½) inches; and for all other devices to be cut in shape of a quadrant of a circle having a radius of from four (4) to six (6) inches (as size of device may require), the straight sides of pieces to be neatly stitched to the under side of the upper edge of cloth of arms; the nap of the cloth to run downward when the chevron is on the sleeve.

The cloth forming the background of devices to be of facing cloth of same color of facings of the uniform coat.

Bars and Arms.—The bars of the chevron to be outlined on the groundwork of facing cloth in rows of heavy stitching of No. 8 silk, the upper and lower edges to be finished with similar stitching.

White stitching for Engineers and overcoats for Infantry, and black for all others.

The arms of the chevron bars to be six (6) to seven (7) inches long, to be the arcs of a circle of about twenty-five (25) inches radius, and to meet at an angle of about ninety-six (96) degrees; distance between extreme outer ends about nine (9) inches.

Designs for Chevrons—Sergeant Major.—Three bars and an arc of three bars. The upper edge of outer bar of arc to be the arc of a circle of about seven and one-fourth (7¼) inches radius.

Quartermaster Sergeant.—Three bars and a tie of three bars. The upper bar of tie to extend horizontally from the extreme outer end of one arm of the chevron to that of the other.

Saddler Sergeant.—Three bars and a saddler's round knife, handle upward. Knife of the following dimensions: handle one and three-fourths (1¾) inches long, three-fourths (¾) inch wide near top; five-eighths (⅝) inch near blade; blade one and one-eighth (1⅛) inches deep in center; from point to point of blade three and one-fourth ($3\frac{1}{4}$) inches; center of edge one and one-fourth ($1\frac{1}{4}$) inches above inner angle of chevron.

Chief Trumpeter.—Three bars and an arc of one bar, with bugle of pattern worn on cap, about one and one-half ($1\frac{1}{2}$) inches above inner angle of chevron. The upper edge of bar of arc to be the arc of a circle of about seven and one-fourth ($7\frac{1}{4}$) inches radius. Bugle to be of form, dimensions, and finish of the standard sample chevron.

Principal Musician.—Three bars and a bugle. The bugle to be the same as for Chief Trumpeter's chevrons.

Ordnance Sergeant.—Three bars and an outlined star. Lower point of star to be about one (1) inch above inner angle of chevron. Star to be of dimensions and finish of standard sample chevron.

Post Quartermaster Sergeant.—Three bars, and a crossed pen and key, embroidered in gold-colored silk. The key and pen to cross about two and one-half ($2\frac{1}{2}$) inches above the inner angle of the chevron, and to be of form, dimensions, and finish of standard sample chevron.

Commissary Sergeant.—Three bars and a crescent (points front). Distance from point to point of crescent, two (2) inches; width in center, three-fourths ($\frac{3}{4}$) of one inch; center of lower edge to be about one and three-fourths ($1\frac{3}{4}$) inches above inner angle of chevron.

Hospital Steward.—Three bars and an arc of one bar, with a red cross placed about one and seven-eighths ($1\frac{7}{8}$) inches above inner angle of chevron. The upper edge of bar to be the arc of a circle of about seven and one-fourth ($7\frac{1}{4}$) inches radius. Cross to be of form, dimensions, and finish of standard sample chevron.

Acting Hospital Steward.—Same as for a Hospital Steward, omitting the arc.

1st Sergeant.—Three bars and an outlined lozenge, having sides about one-fourth ($\frac{1}{4}$) of an inch wide. Lozenge about two and one-half ($2\frac{1}{2}$) inches long and two (2) inches wide, placed lengthwise about one and one-fourth ($1\frac{1}{4}$) inches above inner angle of chevron.

Sergeant.—Three bars.

Regimental and Battalion Color Sergeant.—Three bars and a sphere one-fourth ($\frac{1}{4}$) of an inch wide, one and one-fourth ($1\frac{1}{4}$) inches in outside diameter, and placed one and three-fourths ($1\frac{3}{4}$) inches above inner angle of chevron.

Corporal.—Two bars.

Farrier.—A horseshoe three-fourths (¾) of an inch wide, abont four and one-half (4½) inches long from outer edge of toe-piece to a line between extreme points of heels; between outer lines across center, about three and three-fourths (3¾) inches; between extreme points of heels, about two (2) inches. A toe-piece about one and three-fourths (1¾) inches long, one-half (½) inch deep, and two (2) heel-pieces about one-half (½) by three-fourths (¾) inch each, of gray facing cloth, to be stitched on. Four (4) nail-holes on each side of the shoe, at equal distances from each other, to be underlaid with blue cloth.

Pioneer.—Two (2) crossed axes of the following dimensions: Handles four and one-half (4½) inches long, one-fourth (¼) to one-third (⅓) of an inch wide; axe two (2) inches long and about one (1) inch wide at the edge.

Workmanship.—To be in accordance with standard samples adopted this day.

Adopted June 10, 1889, *in lieu of specifications of January* 27, 1888, *which are hereby canceled.*

S. B. HOLABIRD,
Quartermaster General, U. S. A.

1571—F., 1889.

CHEVRONS.

CLOTH.

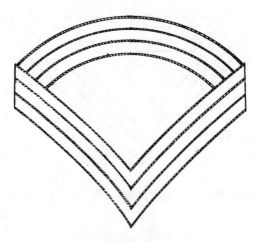

SERGEANT MAJOR.

ORDNANCE SERGEANT.

CHEVRONS.
CLOTH.

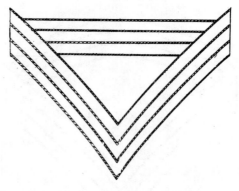

QUARTERMASTER SERGEANT.

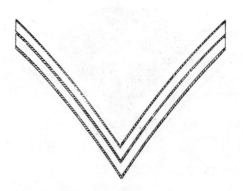

CORPORAL.

CHEVRONS.

CLOTH.

SADDLER SERGEANT.

PIONEER.

CHEVRONS.

CLOTH.

FARRIER.

POST QUARTERMASTER SERGEANT.

CHEVRONS.

CLOTH.

HOSPITAL STEWARD.

ACTING HOSPITAL STEWARD.

CHEVRONS.

CLOTH.

PRINCIPAL MUSICIAN.

CHIEF TRUMPETER.

SERGEANT.

CHEVRONS.

CLOTH.

COMMISSARY SERGEANT.

FIRST SERGEANT.

CHEVRONS.

CLOTH.

REGIMENTAL AND BATTALION COLOR

SERGEANT.

WAR DEPARTMENT,

QUARTERMASTER GENERAL'S OFFICE.

Specifications for Metallic Ornaments for Helmets and Forage Caps.

FOR HELMETS.

Eagles.—Eagle according to pattern, made of No. 24 sheet-brass (high); American eagle displayed proper with national shield on breast and bearing in beak a scroll with motto "E pluribus unum;" olive branch in dexter talon and bunch of arrows in sinister. For troops of the line the distinguishing arms are displayed under the shield, viz.: Artillery, the crossed cannon; cavalry, crossed sabers; infantry, crossed rifles, and upon the lower part of shield is borne the regimental number in German silver. For the staff and staff corps, the crossed arms are omitted and the designating badge, in German silver, is borne upon the lower part of shield, viz.: For post quartermaster sergeants, the crossed pen and key; for the hospital corps, the Geneva cross; for commissary sergeants, the crescent; for engineers, the castle; for ordnance and ordnance sergeants, the shell and flame. When flat the eagle is of about the following dimensions: Greatest width between tips of wings four and one-quarter $(4\frac{1}{4})$ inches; from upper edge of scroll to tip of tail three and seven-eighths $(3\frac{7}{8})$ inches. It shall be molded to the form of helmet shell and be provided with three (3) wire loops by which to fasten it on.

Spike and Base (Foot Troops).—Spike to be of polished high brass, according to pattern, hexagonal, fluted surface, with screw of brass to fit socket in top of helmet. Height of spike three (3) inches; widest diameter one (1) inch; length of screw (in the clear) three-fourths $(\frac{3}{4})$ of an inch; base of No. 24 sheet-brass (high); oak-leaf design according to pattern, eight (8) points, bed in center to receive base of spike and hole cut for spike-screw.

Plume Socket (for Mounted Men's Helmets).—To be of high brass, according to pattern. An inverted fluted cone with mitred top (four points), front ornamented with the national eagle and shield and a single star surmounting eagle head. Spherical base, into the mouth of which the cone is securely brazed, and which is formed into a hexagonal pedestal at the bottom similar to that of spike so as to rest firmly upon the oak-leaf base and be bored for the plume-pin. Height of spherical base (including mouth and pedestal) about one and one-half (1½) inches; of cone two (2) inches; diameter of cone at top one (1) inch, at bottom five-eighths (⅝) of an inch; diameter of spherical base one (1) inch. Plume-pin, with ornamental head and plain washer (each about one and one-fourth (1¼) inches in diameter), about four and three-fourths (4¾) inches in length, the thread of which shall be cut so as to screw into ventilator socket in top of helmet. For the lower end of pin a large open washer or disk with beveled edge to bear against the inside of helmet-shell for the better security of the top piece, and be kept in place by a small brass thumb-nut. Diameter of disk, about two and one-half (2½) inches.

The oak-leaf base to be the same as described for foot helmets.

Side Buttons.—Side buttons to be of high brass, according to pattern, with flat brass double stems. Devices on buttons in relief: For engineers, the castle; for ordnance, the shell and flame; for post quartermaster sergeants, the crossed pen and key; for hospital corps, the Geneva cross of white metal; for commissary sergeants, the crescent; for artillery, the crossed cannon; for cavalry, the crossed sabers; for infantry, the crossed rifles.

Numbers.—Numbers to be one-half (½) inch in height and made of No. 18 German silver, according to pattern, with two soft copper wire stems to hold them on shield.

Devices.—Devices for staff and staff corps to be of German silver, according to patterns. Designs as mentioned in description of eagle, and stems as for numbers.

Scrolls and Rings (Mounted Troops).—Scrolls and rings: One on each side, between the leaf-shaped points of the top piece, its lower edge one-half (½) inch below these points. The scroll is three-fourths (¾) inch diameter, ornamented to correspond with the fastening of the top piece. On the top of the scroll, in the center, is an eye of thin wire three-sixteenths ($\frac{3}{16}$) of an inch high, holding a thin brass ring one-half (½) inch in diameter, to keep the cords and bands in position. The stem of the scroll is formed of two pieces of thin brass wire to fasten it at the inside of helmet. All to be high brass.

FOR FORAGE CAPS.

Bugles for Musicians.—Bugles for field and band musicians: Of sheet-brass (high) No. 28, representing an old-style bugle with circular crook, and a cord slung three (3) fold around the lower part, terminating in two (2) tassels on one, and one (1) tassel on the other side.

Height across crook one and one-fourth ($1\frac{1}{4}$) inches; width from mouth-piece to outer edge of bowl two and one-fourth ($2\frac{1}{4}$) inches. Brass-wire loops same as on letters.

Castles (Engineers).—Castles: Of sheet-brass (high) No. 28, representing an ancient castle with three (3) towers. Height of center tower, seven-eighth ($\frac{7}{8}$) of an inch; of side towers one and one-fourth ($1\frac{1}{4}$) inches each; of battlements between towers five-eighths ($\frac{5}{8}$) of an inch; width at base one and seven-eighths ($1\frac{7}{8}$) inches; at top of side-towers one and three-fourths ($1\frac{3}{4}$) inches. Two brass loops strongly soldered on back to fasten to cap.

Shells and Flames (Ordnance).—Shells and flames: Of sheet-brass (high) No. 28, representing a shell and flame. Diameter of shell three-fourths ($\frac{3}{4}$) of an inch; height of flame from upper edge of shell seven-eighths ($\frac{7}{8}$) of an inch; greatest width of flame one and one-eighth ($1\frac{1}{8}$) inches. Brass-wire loops on back same as on letters.

Wreath and Crescent (Commissary Sergeant).—Wreath: Same as for Post Quartermaster Sergeant; a crescent of German silver, similar to that on helmet eagle, to be worn within the wreath.

Wreaths and Geneva Crosses (Hospital Stewards), and Geneva Crosses without wreaths (Acting Hospital Stewards and Privates Hospital Corps).—Wreaths: Wreath made of German silver, representing two olive branches, held at the bottom by a loop and knot, turning upward and bending in an oval shape, approaching each other at the top. Height one and one-half ($1\frac{1}{2}$) inches; greatest distance between outer edges two and five-eighths ($2\frac{5}{8}$) inches; greatest width of single branch five-eighths ($\frac{5}{8}$) of an inch. Brass-wire loop as on back of letters.

Geneva Crosses.—Of German silver, similar to that on helmet eagle.

Wreaths and crossed Pen and Key (Post Quartermaster Sergeants).—Wreath: Same as above, except that it is made of dead or unburnished gilt metal; a crossed pen and key of German silver, similar to that on helmet eagle, to be worn within the wreath.

Crossed Cannon (Artillery).—Crossed cannon: Of sheet-brass (high) No. 20, representing two cannons crossing each other at the trunnions, muzzle upward; length two and one-eighth ($2\frac{1}{8}$) inches; breadth at breaches two (2) inches; at muzzle one and seven-eighths ($1\frac{7}{8}$) inches. Four brass-wire loops strongly soldered on back to fasten to cap.

Crossed Sabers (*Cavalry*).—Crossed sabers: of sheet-brass (high) No. 20, representing two cavalry sabers in scabbards, crossed in the middle, with hilts and edges upward. To be shaped or curved so as to fit the front of cap. Length of sabers three (3) inches; height from hilt of one to point of other one and one-fourth ($1\frac{1}{4}$) inches; from point to point two and three-fourths ($2\frac{3}{4}$) inches. Four small brass-wire loops same as on crossed cannon.

Crossed Rifles (*Infantry*).—Crossed rifles: Of sheet-brass (high) No. 20; two rifles crossing each other at a point equidistant from the butt and muzzle; muzzles pointing upward and outward; hammers upward, their position crossed, making the upper space form an angle of 137°; length of rifle two and five-eighths ($2\frac{5}{8}$) inches; diameter at point of crossing about one-eighth ($\frac{1}{8}$) of an inch; to be shaped or curved so as to fit the front of cap. The whole ornament occupying a rectangular space of about two and seven-sixteenths ($2\frac{7}{16}$) inches wide by one and three-eighths ($1\frac{3}{8}$) inches high. Fastenings: Four brass-wire loops firmly soldered, opening horizontally with the rifles, and placed about one-half ($\frac{1}{2}$) inch from the muzzles and butts.

Letters "*A*" *to* "*M.*"—Brass letters "A" to "M:" Roman capitals, one-half ($\frac{1}{2}$) inch long, to be made of sheet-brass (high) No. 28; edges beveled. Two small brass-wire loops strongly soldered on the back of letter to fasten it to the cap.

Numbers "1" *to* "o."—Brass numbers: Nos. "1" to "o," inclusive, one-half ($\frac{1}{2}$) inch long, to be made of sheet-brass (high) No. 28; edges beveled. Small brass-wire loops same as on letters.

Adopted July 9, 1889, in lieu of those of March 10, 1888, which are hereby canceled.

S. B. HOLABIRD,
Quartermaster General, U. S. A.

1706—F., 1889.

ORNAMENTS,
METALLIC, FOR HELMETS.
(EAGLES).

CAVALRY.

ARTILLERY.

ORNAMENTS,

METALLIC, FOR HELMETS.
(EAGLES).

STAFF.

INFANTRY.

ORNAMENTS,
METALLIC, FOR HELMETS.

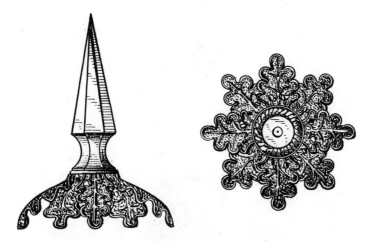

SPIKE AND BASE

PLUME SOCKET AND BASE.

ORNAMENTS,

METALLIC, FOR HELMETS.

SCROLL AND RING.

SIDE BUTTONS.

CAVALRY.   ARTILLERY.   INFANTRY.

ENGINEERS.   ORDNANCE.   COMMISSARY SERGEANT.

POST QUARTERMASTER   HOSPITAL CORPS.   SECTIONAL VIEW.
    SERGEANT.

ORNAMENTS,

METALLIC, FOR HELMETS.

MUSICIANS.

1234567890

NUMBERS.

POST QUARTERMASTER
SERGEANT.

ORDNANCE.

ENGINEERS.

COMMISSARY SERGEANT.

HOSPITAL STEWARD.

ORNAMENTS,

METALLIC, FOR FORAGE CAPS.

ENGINEERS.

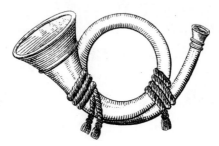

FIELD MUSICIAN.

HOSPITAL STEWARD.

ORNAMENT
METALLIC, FOR FORAGE CAPS.

POST QUARTERMASTER SERGEANT

COMMISSARY SERGEANT

ORNAMENTS
METALLIC, FOR FORAGE CAPS.

ORDNANCE.

ORNAMENTS,
METALLIC, FOR FORAGE CAPS.

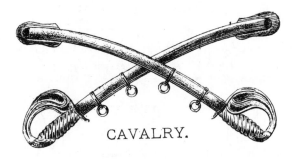

CAVALRY.

ARTILLERY.

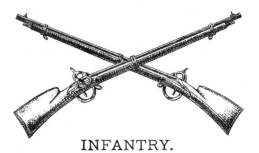

INFANTRY.

ORNAMENTS,

METALLIC, FOR FORAGE CAPS.

BRASS LETTERS.

ABCDEFG
HIKLM

BRASS NUMBERS.

1234567890

Specifications for Summer Sack Coats.

Material.—To be made of white cotton duck, twenty-eight and one-half (28½) inches wide, weighing six and one-half (6½) to seven (7) ounces to the yard, bleached for non-commissioned officers and bandsmen, unbleached for privates.

Pattern.—To be a single-breasted sack coat with falling collar, five (5) button-holes and five (5) eyelet-holes for buttons worked on the front. Buttons to be secured by toggles or split-rings. No pockets or lining. A set of regulation gilt buttons, a set of white vegetable ivory buttons, and a set of toggles or split-rings to be furnished with each coat.

Workmanship:—To be made in accordance with the standard samples and the following sizes:

SIZES No.	Breast Measure.	Waist Measure.	Length of Coat.	Length of Sleeve.	Length of Collar.
	Inches.	*Inches.*	*Inches.*	*Inches.*	*Inches.*
1	36	34	28	31½	17
2	37	35	28½	32½	17½
3	39	37	29	33	18
4	41	39	29½	34	19
5	42	40	30½	34¾	20
6	44	43	31½	35	20¼

Adopted July 5, 1889, in lieu of specifications of September 22, 1888, which are hereby canceled.

S. B. HOLABIRD,
Quartermaster General, U. S. A.

1908—F., 1889.

SUMMER SACK COAT.

WAR DEPARTMENT,

QUARTERMASTER GENERAL'S OFFICE.

Specifications for Summer Trousers.

Material.—To be made of white cotton duck, twenty-eight and one-half (28½) inches wide, weighing six and one-half (6½) to seven (7) ounces to the yard, bleached for non-commissioned officers and bandsmen, unbleached for privates. Pockets and linings of white jeans, and white bone suspender and fly buttons, and white-metal buckle for strap at the back.

Pattern.—To be made with waist-band, regular made slanting top pockets, a watch pocket in the seam on right side, at entrance to regular pocket, and a regular made hip pocket on the right side. Outside seams double stitched, forming a light welt.

Workmanship.—To be made in accordance with the standard samples and the following measurements :

Sizes No.	Waist.	Seat.	Inside Seam.	Outside Seam.	Bottom.
	Inches.	*Inches.*	*Inches.*	*Inches.*	*Inches.*
1	31	36	30½	40½	19½
2	32	38	31	41½	20
3	33	40	32	43½	20½
4	34	42	33	44½	20½
5	36	44	34	45½	21
6	40	45	35	46½	21

Adopted July 5, 1889, in lieu of specifications of September 22, 1888, which are hereby canceled.

Specifications for white linen trousers, adopted August 5, 1885, are hereby canceled.

S. B. HOLABIRD,

Quartermaster General, U. S. A.

1908—F., 1889.

SUMMER TROUSERS

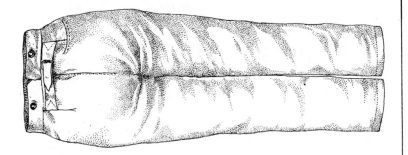

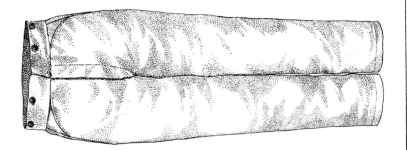

WAR DEPARTMENT,

QUARTERMASTER GENERAL'S OFFICE.

Specifications for Silk and Silk Twist.

Silk.—Black machine silk, size "B." One-ounce spools to contain 750 yards each, to stand a tensile strength of eight (8) pounds; to be of strictly pure dye and clear black color. Spool silk, size "B" on 20 yards, 30 yards, 70 yards, and 100 yard spools, to stand a tensile strength of eight (8) pounds and contain full measurement, and to be of strictly pure dye.

Twist.—Button-hole twist, sizes No. 10, No. 12 and No. 14, on one-ounce spools. Size No. 10 to stand a tensile strength of nineteen (19) pounds, and each spool to contain 312 yards. Size No. 12 to stand a tensile strength of sixteen (16) pounds, and each spool to contain 368 yards. Size No. 14 to stand a tensile strength of fourteen (14) pounds, and each spool to contain 424 yards. Seven (7) yard, ten (10) yard, and twenty-four (24) yard spools to be same size, strength, and quality of twist as the one-ounce spools. All button-hole twist to be of strictly pure dye, a clear black color, and full measurement.

Chevron Silk.—Black and white on one-ounce spools, to stand a tensile strength of twenty-one (21) pounds, and measure 285 yards to the spool.

Raw Stock.—All silk and silk twist to be of best "Tsatlee" or "Japan" raw stock, or other equally good, thoroughly cleaned, free from knots and slugs.

Stamping of Spools, Packing, etc.—All spools of silk or twist to be indelibly stamped on one end of the spool "Property of the United States," and on the other end the quantity and size of silk the spool contains.

The silk to be put up in boxes of one dozen spools, and silk twist in boxes of eight spools, and marked with the name of the contractor and date of contract.

Adopted August 12, 1889, in lieu of those of April 2, 1885, which are hereby canceled.

S. B. HOLABIRD,
Quartermaster General, U. S. A.

2372—F., 1889.

WAR DEPARTMENT,

QUARTERMASTER GENERAL'S OFFICE,

Specifications for Fifes.

To be made of ebony or other suitable wood, polished, and finished on both ends with a nickel-plated or German silver ferrule. To be in three keys, *i. e.,* " B," " C," or " E," each properly attuned, and equal in all respects to the standard sample.

Adopted September 23, 1889.

S. B. HOLABIRD,
Quartermaster General, U. S. A.

2867—F., 1889.

FIFES.

Specifications for Hatchet Slings.

To be made of black harness leather, the body or pocket of the sling to be of one piece of leather cut to the form of the standard sample, thirteen and one-half (13½) inches long, folded and substantially sewed together at the blade end with a strip of the same kind of leather one-half (½) inch wide inserted.

The bottom to be spread at the poll end by the insertion in the seam of two or more layers of leather one-half (½) inch wide, shaved down and reduced as they approach the blade end, giving the bottom of the sling the form of an ax-head.

To be furnished with a carrying strap three-fourths (¾) of an inch wide, made in two parts, one part seventeen (17) inches long finished with a buckle, keeper and shield, the other part forty-three (43) inches long with a band formed from a strap six (6) inches long, placed seven and one-half (7½) inches from the bottom, to receive the handle of the hatchet.

A small strap six and one-half (6½) inches long to be sewed on the back of the pocket and a corresponding strap with buckle and keeper on the front, to secure the hatchet in the pocket.

All stitching to be strong and neat, with the best linen thread well waxed.

To conform in all respects to the standard sample.

Adopted September 23, 1889.

S. B. HOLABIRD,
Quartermaster General, U. S. A.

2867—F., 1889.

HATCHET SLING.

Specifications for Pick-ax Slings.

To be made of black harness leather. The bottom and sides to be cut and formed to correspond to the curves of the top and sides of a pick-ax, and firmly sewed together, one end of one side being sufficiently large, and properly formed to overlap the pointed end of a pick-ax, forming a pocket with closed end for the same, the center of both sides being cut with lapels to cover the eye of the pick-ax, the other end of both sides forming a trough with open end, three (3) inches deep at lapel tapered to one and one-fourth (1¼) inches at outer end, to receive the blade end of the pick-ax.

To be furnished with a leather carrying strap sixty-two (62) inches long, one and one-fourth (1¼) inches wide, made in two parts, the long part forty-eight (48) inches long, the short part fourteen (14) inches long, with buckle and keeper, the long part of the strap to have a leather band formed from a strap one (1) inch wide by eight (8) inches long securely stitched thereto seventeen (17) inches above the lower end of same, to receive the handle of the pick-ax.

The open or trough end of the sling to be furnished with two straps and buckles to secure the pick-ax within the sling, each strap three-quarters (¾) of an inch wide, and one, seven (7) inches long, the other nine (9) inches long. All of the parts constituting the slings to be securely stitched in the best workmanlike manner, and with the best linen thread well waxed.

To conform in all respects to the standard sample.

Adopted September 23, 1889.

S. B. HOLABIRD,
Quartermaster General, U. S. A.

2867—F., 1889.

370

PICK-AXE SLING.

Index

Duck, 12-oz., Cotton, 37

Fifes, 366
Flag Halliards, 30
Flags, Garrison, 24
Flags, Hospital, 168
Flags, Post, 26
Flags, Storm and Recruiting, 28
Flannel, Blouse Lining, 147
Flannel, Canton, 36
Flannel, Cloth-finished Blouse, 82
Flannel, D. B. fine quality, 161
Flannel, D. B. Shirting and Cape Lining, 330

Gauntlets, Leather, 130
Gauntlets, Muskrat, 92
General Guides, 96
Gloves, White Berlin, 10
Gold Lace, 104
Guidons, Artillery, 132
Guidons, Cavalry, 78

Hatchet-helves, 256
Hatchets, Camp, 254
Hatchet-slings, 368
Hats, Fur, Campaign, 290
Helmet Cords and Bands, 160
Helmet Hair Plumes, 159
Helmets, Cork, 2
Helmets, Metalic Ornaments for, 345
Helmets, untrimmed, 292

Jeans, Corset, 192
Jeans, White, 306

Kersey, Sky-blue, fine quality, 102
Kersey, Sky-blue, heavy quality, 116
Kettles, Camp, 270

Leggins, Canvas, 286
Litters, Hand, 236
Lyres, 158

Markers, 96
Mattress Covers, 118
Mattresses, 86
Messpans, 266
Mittens, Canvas, 68
Mittens, Woolen, 72
Mosquito Bars, 62

Music Pouches, 152

Muslin, Unbleached, 276

Overalls, 310
Overcoats, Canvas (blanket lined), 54
Overcoats (Kersey), 332
Overshirts, 56
Overshoes, 278

Padding, Black, 274
Padding, Canvas, 275
Pickaxe Helves, 252
Pickaxes, 250
Pickaxe Slings, 370
Pillow Cases, 142
Pillows, 88
Pillow Sacks, 16
Ponchos, Rubber, 240
Pots, Iron, 268

Shirts, D. B. Flannel, 56
Shoes, Barrack, 288
Shoes, Campaign, Hand-sewed Bottoms, 300
Shoes, Campaign, with partly Machine sewed Bottoms, 121
Shoulder Knots, 156
Shovels, Long Handle, 262
Shovels, Short Handle, 264
Silesia, Black, 277
Silk and Silk Twist, 364
Spades, 258
Spade Slings, 260
Stable Frocks, 6
Stamps, Company Marking, 74
Standards, Cavalry, 136
Stencil Plates, 34
Stockings, Cotton, 50
Stockings, Woolen, 8
Suspenders, 144

Tent Fly, Hospital, 206
Tent Fly, Wall, 212
Tent Pins, 230
Tent Pipe, 64
Tent Poles, Conical Wall, 232
Tent Poles, Hospital, 20
Tent Poles, Improved Common, 120
Tent Poles, Shelter, 23
Tent Poles, Wall, 22
Tents, Common, with Wall, Closed Corners, 219